Poli

and sc

ins

Politics
and social
insight

Francis G. Castles
Faculty of Social Sciences,
the Open University

SAGE Publications
Beverly Hills
California

For information address:

 SAGE PUBLICATIONS, INC.
275 South Beverly Drive,
Beverly Hills, California 90212

Printed in Great Britain

International Standard Book Number 0-8039-0150-X

Library of Congress Catalog Card No. 72-161585

First Printing

To Penny Ann

Contents

Acknowledgments

While assuming complete responsibility for the contents of this book, I would like to thank Dr J. A. A. Stockwin of the Australian National University and Dr David Potter of the Open University for their assistance. I would also like to record my gratitude to Maureen Harriss for her secretarial help and to my wife who read the proofs. Finally, I must acknowledge the kind permission afforded me by the Editor and publishers of *The Australian and New Zealand Journal of Sociology* to reprint a part of my article 'Scientific Methodology and Social Insight: Some Pedagogic Lacunae in The Social Sciences' (April 1970) which appears as the final section of Chapter 3.

Sociology and the discipline of politics

An academic discipline may be defined in one of two alternative ways. Its focus of interest may be located in either a given method of study or a given set of phenomena as an object of study. These alternatives are not necessarily mutually exclusive, but there is a natural tendency for one or other approach to be predominant. To take as an object of study a particular area of human behaviour implies no specific method; only that every conceivable method or perspective appropriate to the illumination of that subject-area should be utilized. In contrast, the refinement of a particular method of study carries with it the implication that it will be used in all those areas where it may promote the advancement of knowledge.

There can be little question that politics as a discipline is of the type that concentrates its attention on a particular area of activity. However, the manner in which this area may be delimited at a given time depends considerably on the methods and perspectives which are currently thought appropriate for the explanation of political data. Thus in an era when politics is chiefly the concern of philosophers the definition of its area of competence comes to include not merely the mechanics of government, but also all those factors relevant to the conscious creation of a polis in which justice, the general will, or the principles of utility reign supreme. Similarly, the historian's attempt to understand the world in terms of unique sequences of events brings to politics a concern with all those elements of human motivation which make the individual create history in his own image.

In recent times, a number of schools of thought within the discipline of politics have arisen, which, without necessarily having that intention, have severely limited the methods and perspectives avail-

able to the discipline. One, which might be called the constitutionalist school has insisted that with the rise of new social science
disciplines, the study of politics must restrict itself to a distinctive
area of human activity, notably that of governmental behaviour.
Although such an approach in no way logically precludes the utilization of a very wide variety of differing perspectives, the desire to
preserve the integrity of the discipline of politics from the encroach-
ments of other equally sharply defined disciplines in reality leads to
an emphasis that political activity, and governmental activity in
particular, can be explained from the very limited set of data pertain-
ing to formal governmental institutions and a small number of other
bodies, like political parties, clearly oriented in their behaviour to
such institutions.

Another school, that commonly denoted by the term behaviouralist, introduces a further limitation by insisting that a dispassionate
and highly empirical method, suggested to be the essence of science
per se, is the only one appropriate to the study of political activity.
The contention made by this school that the only way of searching
into and discovering truth lies in a method 'deriving from the senses
and particulars, rising by gradual and unbroken ascent, so that it
arrives at the most general axioms last of all' is by no means novel
in the history of science, but has come to politics as a result of the
recent development of data-gathering techniques.[1] Without for a
moment disputing the relevance of behavioural methods in political
studies, an exclusively empiricist approach must limit the use of
theoretical models, much more what Ruskin called 'noble abstraction,'
in the discipline.[2]

That the restrictions introduced by these schools are unacceptable
to many who study politics is testified to by the tardiness of political philosophers in accepting their oft predicted demise, and the
noticeable resurgence of historical studies in politics.[3] Furthermore,
the progressive emergence of sociology as an integral part of political
studies illustrates that once more the area circumscribed by the
discipline is expanding. This essay constitutes an attempt to show the
relevance of sociology in widening the perspectives and methods of the
study of government and politics. To do this may seem unnecessary
in light of the many surveys of the relevance of political sociology
(even though most of them have been produced by one man:
Seymour Martin Lipset), but one of our major points will be that
political sociology as currently practised shares many of the features
of the limiting schools previously mentioned.

Politics and society

The importance of non-governmental factors for the explanation of political reality may perhaps best be illustrated by a paradigm of studies commonly conducted under the rubric of political studies.

Governmental and non-governmental aspects of study in politics

Formal Structure	*Relationship of Formal Structure to Wider Social Reality*
1 The DESCRIPTION of formal GOVERNMENTAL institutions (Focus on: legislature, executive, judiciary, etc.)	2 The DESCRIPTION of POLITICAL institutions* (Focus on: political parties, pressure groups, factions, etc.)
3 The ANALYSIS of factors shaping formal GOVERNMENTAL institutions	4 The ANALYSIS of factors shaping POLITICAL institutions
Type of study (Focus on: a. Power b. Bureaucracy Levels of analysis: A. Empirical B. Theoretical)	(Focus depending on level of analysis: A. Empirical B. Theoretical a. Ideology b. Class c. Elites C. Metatheoretical a. Functional models b. Conflict models c. Anomic models)
5 The EVALUATION OF THE DESIRABILITY of formal GOVERNMENTAL institutions (Focus on: the reform of governmental apparatus)	6 The EVALUATION OF THE DESIRABILITY of POLITICAL institutions (Focus on: the reform of polity and society and the relationship between them)

A number of important issues emerge from even the most cursory examination of this model. Of interest is the fact that in stressing the relationship of the formal governmental structure to the wider social reality no attempt has been made to adopt a fully inclusive definition

* The use of the term POLITICAL in this paradigm is not intended to imply that formal governmental institutions are not political; rather the implication is that the institutions described as POLITICAL cannot in any exclusive sense be seen as governmental in nature. They are politically relevant despite this.

of political studies. The intention of the paradigm was merely to show that a study of government in isolation from all other elements of social structure was rather like *Hamlet* without the Prince of Denmark. Much the same might be said for the relevance of other social science disciplines to politics. The nature of governmental activity is as much bound up in the operation of economic institutions as it is in social ones, and it would almost certainly be possible to construct a similar paradigm to express that relationship. Naturally, one would not expect all disciplines to be as relevant to political explanation as these. There can, however, be no *a priori* assumption that the perspectives and methods of a particular discipline are inappropriate. Only the attempt to use them and their subsequent failure could justify such a conclusion.[4] The use of biological and psychological perspectives might be thought inappropriate in politics, since both disciplines deal with invariants of human behaviour, and the major task of politics may be taken as the explanation of varying forms of political behaviour. However, the superimposition of variable behaviour on a fixed sub-stratum of animal or human disposition may itself serve to explain some otherwise obscure aspects of political activity.[5]

What is most striking about the paradigm as presented is that none of the logical ways of cutting-in on the subject-matter offer anything like a coherent or sufficient approach to the study of politics. This is true not merely in terms of the labels offered in the model, but also in terms of the nomenclature adopted by those who profess to teach the discipline. The notable example of this is, of course, in departments with the appellation of 'government'. By any normal definition, the word government must be regarded as largely synonymous with those elements of study designated under the rubric of formal structure. One might expect such a department to concentrate its energies on the description, analysis and evaluation of the formal institutions of government. But it is very unlikely that any department did this, even in the heyday of the constitutionalist school, much less today. On the one side, these elements of study, all presumably necessary for a satisfactory explanation of governmental behaviour, have not been accorded an equal status. As was also true of the beginnings of sociology, those who attempted to create politics as a discipline clearly separate from others, did so by a method of classification leading to a vastly disproportionate emphasis on simple description.[6] For example, although it is arguable that classification must precede analysis, in politics the emphasis was such that it is only recently that a realization has come about that a cogent analysis of factors shaping governmental institutions may stem from a general understanding of the dynamics of organizations, rather than from a meticulous description of particular administrative practices.[7]

On the other side is the fact that, despite nomenclature and the effort to preserve the integrity of government as a separate study, departments of government have never been able to neglect completely the relationship of formal structures to the wider social reality. Those groups, which contemporary political scientists describe as input structures, political parties, pressure groups and factions, could not be ignored, simply because without looking at them, there was no way to explain how and for whom government performed its functions. Political parties do not merely translate the demands of the individual, shaped as they are by his position in the social structure, but without their explanatory power it is impossible to understand any given decision that comes from governmental structures like parliament and cabinet. Furthermore, with the notable exception of the behaviouralists, no school within the discipline of politics has succeeded in extirpating the influence of political philosophy conceived as the evaluation of the desirability of political institutions. The explanation of this is quite straightforward in that political philosophy introduced a wider social understanding through the back door. There were very few philosophical interpreters of political activity who did not realize the crucial relevance of the nature of social life to the form of government. Certainly the sociologists who may claim to have removed the evaluative content from such analytical concepts as class, ideology and elite cannot be so presumptuous as to describe themselves as their progenitors. All are to be discovered in the long history of political philosophy, and the primacy in introducing concepts like 'political socialization' cannot be attributed to American political scientists, but to Plato's seminal discussion of the upbringing of the Guardians.

The behaviouralists are only able to avoid the exigency of utilizing political philosophy to emphasize the relationship of the formal governmental structure to social existence as a whole because they do not in the first place attempt to make any artificial distinction between social and political facts. Their attitude is aptly put by Heinz Eulau who suggests that:

A study of politics which leaves man out of its equations is a rather barren politics. Yet such is the propensity of man that he can consider his own creations without measuring them by himself. Political science has studied political ideas, values, customs, symbols, institutions, processes and policies without reference to their creators for a long time . . .[8]

considered desirable without inquiring whether their ethical imperatives were possible to achieve. Equally, the most modest reform of
the governmental structure depends for its effectiveness on an adequate delineation of the structure of government and an analysis of
the factors shaping it. It was as a practitioner of politics in its most
inclusive formulation, the art of the possible, that Marx devoted his
life to proving that a classless society was a viable form of social
organization, and that consequently the 'truly human' society which
he desired might be achieved. The only problem with political
philosophy's claim to independence is that raised in the discussion of
those who wish to restrict the focus of the discipline of politics to the
formal institutions of government. Although probably the political
philosopher utilizes a wider range of perspectives than his constitutionalist colleague, he introduces limitations to the discipline to the
degree that he too is unwilling to admit explicitly his reliance on the
findings and perspectives of other disciplines.

Political sociology and the sociology of politics

In terms of the paradigm offered, it appears sensible to delineate as
political sociology all those areas of study which relate the formal
governmental structure to the wider social environment within which
it operates. However, once more the illogic of academic specialization
operates, and the lines of inquiry pursued by the study appear to be
largely coterminous with elements 2, 3 and 4 of the paradigm.[13] The
avoidance of the evaluation of the desirability of political institutions
derives from sociology's almost neurotic fear of being thought unscientific, and its identification of prescriptive theory with all that is
unscientific. On the other hand, political sociology's major pre-
occupation with power and the dynamics of governmental organization can be explained by an academic analogy to the physical law
that nature abhors a vacuum. As suggested earlier, it is only com-
paratively recently that political scientists realized that the 'science
of administration' was more than an excuse for a detailed exegesis
of administrative practice, and in their absence the sociologists to
a large extent made the area their own preserve. Moreover, sociology's take-over bid was not without justification in academic terms.
All organizations have much in common in virtue of the imperative
co-ordination which facilitates their decision-making function, and
there is no obvious reason why governmental organizations should
not be analysed in the same way as other organizations.
    The claims this essay has made for the relevance of sociology
in illuminating a wide range of socially structured constraints in-
fluencing the political process in all its aspects is, of course, reiterated

by those describing themselves as political sociologists. Lewis Coser, for instance, makes the same point with an analogy, which perhaps implicitly overstates the role of sociological explanation in politics:

'One may say that political science (this term being more or less synonymous with the study of formal structures) has tended to concentrate on the visible part of the political iceberg whereas political sociology has paid greater attention to the submerged portions.'[14] However, political sociology, as many of its contemporary practitioners see its scope, is far more limited in its relevance to political studies than one might imagine. It is very frequently less a sociology of politics, than a borrowing of a certain methodology which has found favour with some sociologists.

This methodology is that empiricism which Bacon so favoured, and which, in an extreme form, C. Wright Mills excoriated as 'abstracted empiricism'.[15] Clearly, the various techniques of empirical investigation are quite essential for accurately describing social and political reality, and for testing hypotheses in both areas, but the disproportionate emphasis on them, so frequently found in modern political sociology, can lead to a neglect of the more theoretical perspectives offered by the mainstream of sociological thought, or to mere triviality. This latter is, of course, one of the most pointed criticisms Mills makes of that branch of political necromancy which is today dignified with the title of psephology.[16] As he says:

> It must be interesting to political scientists to examine a
> full-scale study of voting which contains no reference to
> party machinery for 'getting out the vote', or indeed to any
> political institutions.[17]

A large number of voting studies today presents exactly the same sort of interest.[18] That triviality should not be attributed to psephologists alone is illustrated by the following summary of findings relating to the correlates of the individual's activism in politics.

> Clearly the thinkers are also the doers; those who have an
> interest in politics and tend to pay attention to political
> matters in the mass media and discuss political matters with
> their friends and relatives are also more likely to be active
> in political affairs than those who pay little attention to, and
> have little involvement in, matters political.[19]

Perhaps all this is a little unfair to political sociology; triviality occurs in all disciplines, but its danger is perhaps greatest in those which confuse their methodology with the substance of their study. Much more serious is the disemphasis on theoretical perspectives that may follow in the wake of an empiricist approach. This is not

an area where categorical judgments can be made; the list of individual and eminent political sociologists whose writings bring
to politics a sophisticated reinterpretation of classical sociological
theory is by no means short. Among the obvious examples would be
Lipset's work on the prerequisites of political stability, which carries
on the great tradition of De Tocqueville's *Democracy In America,* or
Raymond Aron's fascinating reworking of Pareto's elitist thesis.[20]
Despite the existence of such important theorists in the field, the
impression political sociology conveys is not one of theoretical
acumen. In the area of community power studies, for instance, the
dominant perception is of a vast collection of empirical studies, all
of them utilizing somewhat different research methods to ask the
simple question, who holds the reins of power. Few of them betray
much awareness of the enormous complexities of the concept of power,
explored by theorists like Marx, Weber and Parsons, and fewer still
appear to realize that in looking at the 'pure, unalloyed, facts', the
methods used to uncover the real power-holders may lead to pre-
judgment and the conversion of the investigation into a self-
fulfilling prophecy. Certainly, this latter criticism may be applied to
the reputational approach to community leadership, since to ask a
progressively diminishing, and largely self-recruited, group of reputed
influentials who are the ten major leaders in the community, will
almost inevitably lead to the conclusion that there exists a small,
coherent and self-aware elite.[21] Since each method adopted of
measuring community power seems to lead to a somewhat different
model of influence, and since, in any case, all the studies are carried
out in relatively small towns, where the application of rigidly
empirical methods is possible, the picture that emerges of the power
structure of the country as a whole is less than impressive.

This lack of theoretical perspective in political sociology manifestly does not come from an unawareness of the relevance of sociology to the discipline of politics. Nor, certainly, does it stem from
an absence of a continuing tradition of theoretical speculation in
sociology, rather it appears to be the result of a differential visibility
of theory and method in contemporary sociology as perceived by
those who borrow from that discipline. What the political scientist
who recognizes the relevance of the social context of politics and
ipso facto sociology receives from his new discipline by adoption is a
clearly thought out empirical method and a set of accepted concepts,
which are regarded less as theoretical tools capable of almost infinite
refinement than as convenient labels for political as well as social
behaviour. Concepts, like class and ideology, are seen not as dynamic
means of analysis but as tags which serve to identify the empirical
regularities uncovered by empirical research. Studies rarely set out

to test which of a number of varying, and often ambiguous, concepts derived from a single theoretical edifice are most likely 'to reduce the empirical bearing upon research of the logical fallacy of affirming the consequent'.[22] In other words, political sociologists take concepts from sociology as received wisdom and are rarely willing to subject them to testing. Even where, as in Dahl's attempt to relate, and test, a number of theories about power structure to the process of decision-making, this is done, the effort may once more be vitiated by a method which introduces pre-judgment of results.[23]

This problem, that political sociology takes from sociology only certain highly visible elements, and not all those perspectives that would be available to a general sociology of politics, is almost certainly pedagogic in nature. Basically, and as T. S. Eliot argued so cogently, '*A cat is not a dog*.'[24] In other words, the majority of political sociologists are not sociologists. This is not to say that if they were exclusively sociologists it would be of any help. The point is that made by those who advocate an inter-disciplinary approach to the social sciences, they must be both sociologists and political scientists. The process of role induction as a professional in either field is not one of learning given methods and certain concepts in isolation. The courses offered by the different disciplines in the history of political thought and the history of sociological theory provide a learning process for the student comparable to that experienced by a child inducted into a given culture. Not everything learnt has immediate utility, rather his culture provides him with a fund of knowledge which functions to give him an orientation to the existential world in which he finds himself. This sensitization to the world of experience is precisely what is offered by those noble abstractions, or metatheoretical conceptions, which, while they are so rarely amenable to testing, function as a back-drop to all academic endeavour, whether conceptual or empirical. It is precisely this induction into the wider culture of sociology that so many political sociologists lack, and which if the full range of sociological perspectives are ever to be utilized in the study of politics, the discipline of politics must in some way provide.

The elementary forms of the political life

Politics as social interaction

The introductory chapter on sociology and the discipline of politics argued that contemporary practitioners of that discipline should give greater emphasis to social parameters in their explanation of political behaviour, and that such explanation, even where it does take account of factors of this kind, is frequently deficient in theoretical acumen. It was suggested, moreover, that these gaps in the fabric of political studies might only be overcome by an induction into that fund of knowledge provided by the wider culture of sociology. A first step in this induction process may be taken by examining the relevance of the most elementary components of society to the study of politics.

On first sight, the most obvious candidate for the basic building-block of a science of society is the individual human being. All social and political activities are undertaken in the last instance by individual men, whether or no they act in concert. But in reality, to adopt such an approach would be untrue to the nature of the subject-matter in which we are interested. Social action is by definition other-regarding action. The word social, and with it the word society, means in conjunction with other men. Consequently, the basic unit of social analysis must be one which includes this other-regarding aspect of man's activity; it must deal, not so much with the actions of individual human beings, but with the *interactions* between them, or rather, as Weber points out, it may deal with individuals, but only insofar as their actions take others into account. This distinction may be illustrated by an example from that writer. As he suggests, 'social action is not identical either with the similar actions of many persons or with action influenced by other persons'.[1] For instance, if a large number of individuals react to a rainstorm by putting up umbrellas, they are not involved in any social interaction, but in a number of individual reactions to a non-human stimulus. On the other hand, if their motivation for sheltering from the rain in this manner is a desire not to appear ludicrous before their fellows such action would have the status of other-regarding activity. This example, among other things, illustrates the importance of an understanding of individual motivations in analysing social phenomena. Dependent on the individual's motivation is the whole significance of his act.

While other-regarding action by an individual is essential for an act to be social it is not sufficient. The umbrella-raiser may be motivated by the desire not to appear silly in the eyes of his fellows, but in fact they may not regard his action or lack of it as significant in any respect. In other words, to them umbrella-raising is neither a sign of silliness or its opposite; to them it is a matter of supreme indifference. We must consequently modify our statement that other-regarding action constitutes social action by the caveat that this is only the case when others regard the action as one of significance. A true definition of social action is one in which there is implied a reciprocity of interaction. The fact that a reciprocity of interaction is implied by the word social is the reason that rather than regard the single individual as the basic social unit, Simmel's view must be endorsed that 'the simplest sociological formation, methodologically speaking, remains that which operates between two elements'.[2] If a man by himself is not a social entity, neither can he be *homo politicus*. Politics necessarily involves the exercise of power, and to have power over anything other than inanimate nature, means the establishment of an interaction in which one individual's actions are other-regarding in the sense of asserting a claim to obedience and others regard that assertion as significant, whether or no they are willing to accord it legitimacy. If, as is often suggested, it was only when Robinson Crusoe found Man Friday that a social existence could begin, it is equally true that only with the latter's arrival could an assertion of white supremacist values be made and with it the beginnings of a reign of political normalcy.

Even at the basic level of the simplest sociological formation a wide range of possible types of social interaction may be isolated. As John Rex has pointed out, there exist three ideal typical possibilities in the interaction between two individuals.[3] These he calls perfect co-operation, perfect conflict, and perfect anomie.

A situation of perfect co-operation between two individuals may be exemplified by the following situation:

Imagine two friends who have been so related for some time. The actions of each when they are together are mutually adapted. After a while each can, as we say, 'count upon' the other. In fact it is not merely that A can guess what B will do, as a psychiatrist can guess at the likely response of his patient, and it is not merely that B can guess what A will do, as indeed the patient may guess at the likely conduct of the psychiatrist. There is more to it than that. A knows that B knows what A is likely to do, and B knows what A expects B to expect. Something which one can call a mutually accepted system of expectations gets established . . .[4]

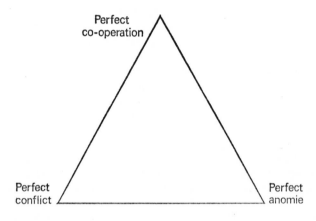

This situation of mutual adaptation which can occur in families, friendships, economic firms, total societies, and even, rarely, in the relationships between nation states, constitutes one sub-type of the simplest sociological formation. Ignoring for the moment the question of whether co-operation can ever be total, it should be noted that co-operation between two actors can be limited to defined spheres. Nation states are capable of co-operative endeavour in time of war without any implied co-operation in other areas, such as fostering each other's economic systems. There are in fact accepted methods of symbolizing a willingness to co-operate on a limited scale. Lévi-Strauss illustrates a co-operative mechanism in the limited interaction of customers at lower-priced restaurants in the south of France. Here the customers, even if they are strangers to each other, exchange the small carafes of wine which come with their meals to symbolize their willingness to co-operate within the degree of intimacy imposed by sharing a meal at a single table.[5]

But if, rather than accepting the proffered carafe of wine, it is rejected, we find a situation in which conflict exists. A may know precisely what B expects of him, but nonetheless not wish to comply with those expectations.[6] Where A and B are perfectly well aware of each other's expectations, but are equally unwilling to take action to fulfil those expectations, a situation of perfect conflict exists. Two examples taken from the sphere of wage bargaining may serve to illustrate the distinction between co-operative and conflict types of interaction. In the period 1949–50, the Swedish trade unions initiated a voluntary wage stop in face of threatened inflation. In these circumstances, when trade union and government negotiators met their interaction was based on a common expectation that each would subordinate his particularistic demands to a common necessity for national stringency. However, in a situation of the type described, where inflation is rampant, the more normal reaction is for the government side to preach wage restraint and the trade unions, conscious of the diminishing value of their members' pay-packets, to demand commensurate wage increases. It is not, in the second case, that the negotiators do not understand each other's expectations, but that their expectations are irreconcilably in conflict.

The third possibility, that of perfect anomie, arises, if, instead of accepting or rejecting the expectations made of him by B, A does not understand what is expected of him. If a foreigner sat at the restaurant table in the south of France, he might well not know how to react to the proffered bottle of wine. In doing so, he might offend without the slightest intention. It is, of course, possible that the Englishman might extricate himself from this situation by remembering some of the customs of his own society that are very similar. Buying successive rounds of drinks at the pub seems to serve exactly the same function as exchanging wine. Neither have an economic purpose, since in theory, at least, one gets an exactly similar quantity of refreshment whether one buys one's own or participates in some sort of reciprocal exchange. The purpose of the ritual is manifestly to display a limited friendliness and co-operation. To return to the subject of anomie, this is then a situation which occurs when A and B are each unable to comprehend what the other expects of him, and so are unable to comply with those expectations.

It will be clear that no relationship or set of relationships can possibly constitute an example of one of these perfect types of interaction in its pure form. In effect perfect conflict and perfect anomie both constitute those limiting cases where any relationship or interaction cease to exist. Where two individuals have nothing in common at all, and all their ideals and interests are opposed, they are more likely to kill each other than negotiate. In the political sphere, the nearest approach to such a situation is civil war, where the causes of conflict are sufficient to overcome previous bonds of national identity. In fact, negotiation is itself based on the presupposition of at least a minimum of common expectations. For instance, in the case of the trade union negotiations with government already cited there is an assumption on both sides that such disputes should be resolved without resort to force. Again a social relationship cannot be maintained where both participants are entirely unable to comprehend each other's demands. An example of how a society may decline, or even be physically extinguished, under these circumstances is provided by the tragedy of the aboriginal inhabitants of Tasmania. The demands of the Western 'civilization' with which they were confronted, and whose rules they were forced to obey, were so totally alien to them that in effect they gave up the desire to live either as social or individual beings. They became totally apathetic, the birth-rate declined, and they finally died out. This should serve as a reminder of the great strength of social ties. Deprived of their traditional way of life, the aborigines had no desire to perpetuate their race. Anomie does not usually go this far. To stress the importance of this type of interaction in a society is to make a comparison. It is to suggest that certain situations are more conducive to confusions and misapprehensions of social expectations than others. It is, for instance, to say with Durkheim that, since both depression and economic prosperity bring in their wake a weakening of social ties, one can expect an increase in suicide rates at such periods.[7] Equally, in discussing conflict, our statements have a comparative, rather than absolute, status. Some societies and relationships exhibit more conflict than others; for instance, societies with a wide, perceived, gap between extremes of wealth and poverty have an high probability of overt conflict, whereas those without such a perception will have a lesser incidence.[8] But, if in the real world conflict and anomie are never absolute, neither is co-operation. There was never a friendship in which some slight disagreement did not take place, nor an alliance in which one of the partners did not feel some advantage was being taken of it. Even a relationship as 'special' as that between the United States and Britain can be at least temporarily disturbed by sending troops to Suez or buses to Cuba.

From what has been said so far, it would seem reasonable to conclude that sociology is the study of social interaction, or to rephrase the same point, the study of social relationships. This has indeed been the conclusion of many of those who have studied social phenomena. If it is correct, the applicability of sociological analysis to the study of political and governmental spheres becomes self-evident. It may be that political phenomena constitute a viable field of study, but it is obvious that it is one that is full of sociological interest. Every act of political analysis may also be regarded as an analysis of social interaction, whether it be the interaction between voter and constituency representative, back-bench M.P. and cabinet minister or civil servant and member of the public. The objective of the political sociologist is to try and uncover those factors which condition this interaction and which make it one of co-operation, conflict or anomie. It could be argued, that, while this was true, we might analyse those interactions which were exclusively political under the title of political studies, and leave other types of interaction to the sociologist. While, in a sense, this is not impossible, it has inherent dangers. It is reasonable to make the presumption that the interactions of individuals are quite likely to be similar in kind whether they occur in a political, an economic, a religious, or any other context. There are manifestly struggles for power in the hierarchy of the Church and the business firm just as there are in the arena of national or international politics. To ignore the possibility that conclusions about the nature of social relationships may on occasion be carried over from one context of study to another is only to make the task of the social sciences that much harder. It means, for instance, that every study of small groups and every conclusion drawn from it has to be repeated by the political scientist. Even the most cursory examination of sociological studies of leadership in small groups indicates their possible applicability to political situations. Redl's analysis of the initiatory act in the contest of the class-room situation, where the tension between the demands of the patriarchal teacher and the desires of the children produces circumstances in which the act of a single child in defying the teacher can start an outburst against the teacher, constitutes a single example.[9] At least, on the surface, this seems analogous to the situation where a mob gathers outside the presidential palace, and the violent action of one of its members initiates a riot or revolution. By stressing the unity of sociology as the general study of social interactions, it is possible to utilize insights, like this one gained from the study of primary groups, in order to set up hypotheses, which may be tested in a more specifically political context.

Politics and the moral order

Before it can be regarded as firmly established that the basic building-block of sociological analysis is the social relationship or interaction, a final point must be considered. It was previously suggested that the individual human being could not be taken as such a basic component, since by himself he has no characteristics which are essentially social.

But frequently it has been maintained that the analysis of social interaction must in logic be reducible to the actions of the various individuals involved.[10] Such a contention appears to be self evident. Every group, whether it be composed of two or two million, takes actions, and these actions are solely the resultant of the aggregate of individual behaviour manifested. From this would seem to stem the conclusion that the analysis of individual activity is sufficient for the understanding of all types of human activity; once we understand the individual, we understand everything. This view, in effect reduces sociology to psychology, and, were it accepted, the title of this work might well be changed to *The Psychology of Politics*.

There are, however, a number of reasons why such psychological reductionism must be rejected. Most crucially, sociologists have insisted that social interaction can create a reality above and beyond what each individual brings to the relationship. This can be illustrated by considering what happens when the simplest sociological formation is made more complex by the addition of a third individual. The classic example is offered by Simmel's discussion of the triad of arbitration.[11] This situation occurs when two partners to a dispute decide that a third individual shall settle the matter on objective grounds. In doing so, the disputants give up their right of final decision, and project it not on a man, the arbitrator, but on a rule that both shall obey, in this case the rule of objective judgment. In other words, social interaction has in this case resulted in a rule, or as the sociologist calls it, a *norm*, which may affect their future conduct. Such a norm is an emergent property of the system of interaction, and there seems no more reason to deny its reality than that of the psychological states of the individuals concerned in making it. Another example may serve to clarify this point. Let us imagine once more the two friends we cited as an instance of mutual adaptations. These friends spend much of their time in each other's company, and, in particular, they utilize their free evening in a ritual imbibition at the local hostelry. However, one of them may receive an invitation to a dinner party at a time which coincides with their usual inebriated revelry. He is then in the quandary, that while he may wish to accept the invitation, he will feel guilty about letting down his friend. In individual terms, he is only fulfilling his desire to accomplish the most desirable of two mutually exclusive objectives. But in sociological terms. it can be seen that his guilt stems from contravening a norm, an expectation, imposed on him by his previous social interaction. This fact, that continued social interaction generates normative rules which impose obligations on the individual irrespective of his inclinations, was to Durkheim the defining characteristic of social rather than psychological reality. To him:

> A social fact is to be recognized by the power of external
> coercion which it exercises or is capable of exercising over
> individuals, and the presence of this power may be recognized
> in its turn either by the existence of some specific sanction
> or by the resistance offered against every individual that
> tends to violate it.[12]

Moreover, the farther one moves from examples set in the small
group context, the more one sees man-made rules as social obligations constraining the individual from outside. This is particularly
true of the subject-matter of politics and government, the laws which
man makes, but cannot break at will. Indeed, from this point of view,
we might regard political facts as social facts *par excellence*, insofar
as the ordinances of government, and the political processes which
contribute to them, can be considered as codifications of, and devices
for the conscious creation of, social obligations backed by the full
panoply of the law. It has, in fact, been the task, and major theme,
of that branch of political studies represented by political philosophy
to ask how a situation may be justified in which man-made laws may
be used to constrain some classes of men. Democratic theory itself
provides one such justification in suggesting that such constraints
are not inimical to freedom to the degree that men obey laws which
they have themselves sanctioned, either directly or through elections.
   But the laws enacted through the political process are but one
instance of the sort of norms by which our behaviour is constrained
and which makes it distinctively social. Religious observance has its
norms which must be observed by those who are of the faithful. The
dispute over birth control in the Catholic Church is a dispute over
norms, but it is also a manifestation of the way in which the rules
created by social interaction in the institution we call the Church can
prevent man from following his inclinations. Although never taken
too seriously, the Christian church's normative injunction to avoid
the 'seven deadly sins' might be taken by a cynic, or a sociologist, as
a normative rule expressly designed to prevent man indulging any
of his inclinations. Economic institutions and educational institutions are as capable as religious groups of generating procedures,
which despite the fact that they were originally created by a concert
of minds now act as exterior rules imposed on men. A university
Senate may decide on a rule excluding any student with less than
fifty per cent in his examination results from participating farther in
the life of the university. The day may come, however, when one or
a number of them wish to make an exception for someone in extra-
ordinary circumstances. But the norm they created now stands over
above them; it is an accepted rule of conduct which they cannot

abrogate unilaterally. There is, in other words, a large class of facts which cannot be reduced to individual actions, and these facts are social precisely because they are generated through, and only through, social interaction. The sphere of obligation, and consequently the sphere of the moral, is the creation of the interacting social group and not of the individual, except insofar as he is obliged to obey its dictates. As Fallding says: 'While one person may assert his interests over those of another, no person assumes a moral entitlement over another—but the group does, and a single person may do so if the group makes him its agent.'[13]

This analysis of the way in which social interaction generates normative rules provides a further perspective by which perfect co-operation, conflict and anomie may be viewed. Perfect co-operation is that situation in which all parties to a social relationship hold common norms. Perfect conflict occurs when social actors hold mutually antagonistic norms to be valid, and perfect anomie is that situation in which the individual finds himself entirely without normative directives. Anomie may be described as normlessness; where the individual in his action is unable to find sufficient guidance from social expectations. This individual condition is a result of either a superfluity of normative demands current in the individual's social situation, with a resulting confusion of what is expected of him, or a weakening of normative imperatives in his social milieu.[14]

The structuring of political action

A social interaction between two individuals is, taken by itself, a very simple and ephemeral structure. However, such interactions are the basic components of groupings varying in size from the nuclear family of father, mother and child, to the nation state of many millions. There is, moreover, a tendency for relationships to acquire some degree of permanence and formal structuring. This is implicit in the individual's need to have his expectations of others fulfilled. This is exemplified in the marriage contract, which is a part of the normative regulation surrounding the family group. A man and woman could live together exactly as they did when married without any ceremony taking place. However, under such circumstances, neither party would have any guarantee of the other's continued adherence to their expectations of a continued life together. It is the norms surrounding the act of marriage which to some extent provide that guarantee. Like the other norms, we have mentioned, it has an external force against the individuals who have voluntarily participated in it. It not only conditions and regulates the manner of family life (the wife shall 'love, honour and obey'), but also institutes penalties for the non-fulfilment of the conditions of the contract (the payment of alimony). The rules by which business and governmental organizations are conducted have the same function; because they are permanent, they make it possible for the individual to interact with others in a consistent manner.[15] With permanence also goes structure. Any set of individuals who wish to prolong an ephemeral interaction into a more permanent group will again, because they wish to know where they stand, elaborate the responsibilities of each individual concerned. Such rules about who does what and when, are as much norms as any of the other types of regulation already discussed, and they are just as capable of creating obligations. For instance, within the British family, the man is supposed to be the bread-winner, and the wife, the guardian of home and children. During the Great Depression, however, the man was often unable to carry out the obligations imposed by the structure of the family through no fault of his own, and in consequence his stature within the family was frequently diminished.

Interactions of more than two individuals have another feature which is indicative of the existence of a social reality above and beyond the summation of individual characteristics. This lies in the fact that the survival of a group is independent of the survival of its individual members. Imagine a group of three members, A, B and C. If C leaves the group and another individual, D, joins it on the express condition that he maintains the original rationale of the group interaction, whatever it may be, then the group still exists. Although the personnel of the British army has changed more than somewhat in the last fifty years, it is still the British army. To deny this is to fall once more into the trap of reducing everything into individual components. An army is not just composed of hundreds of individuals, and its actions cannot be determined by a minute analysis of their predispositions. An army is composed of soldiers, and the role of soldier can only be defined in relation to the whole set of normative regulations and traditions which surround military activity. A man may be a coward and the laws of his country may force him into the army. Once there, he is hedged around with all sorts of norms which dictate how a 'proper' soldier behaves, and the result may be that the man, whose psychological dispositions and rational self-interest would make him run away in the face of the enemy, ends up with a medal for gallantry.

If it is true that ephemeral social interaction tends to become concretized in structured groups, we have noted that, inseparably with such development, there comes a development of a complex of established norms which regulate group activity. This complex may be referred to as a *social institution*.[16] Very often this term is used interchangeably with *group*, but there are good reasons why they should be distinguished. One such is the already noted fact that particular groups may, because of conflict or anomic interactions within them, fail to conform to the pattern of normatively expected behaviour. The social institution of marriage prescribes that husband and wife will cleave to one another till death do them part, but the divorce statistics indicate that concrete family groups may diverge from this norm. Moreover, any group, even if its conformity to social norms is absolute, will tend to develop unique features which differentiate it from the general pattern. Thus, while the norms surrounding marriage include the care of children, the details of such care are not prescribed and may well vary from family to family.The same arguments apply to the need to distinguish between the concrete groups of government and political party and the social institution of constitutional law which regulates their activity. The governments of some nations have been known to depart from the spirit and letter of their constitutions, and certainly every government has unique features which differentiate it from previous groups of men that have undertaken the governmental task.

It has already been noted that the elaboration of a structured and permanent group involves its constituent individuals taking on differential rights and obligations. That this should be the case follows from the logic of group co-operation. It saves the time and energy of every member of the group if every member specializes in one facet of their activity to the exclusion of other considerations. The most famous exemplification of this principle can be seen in Adam Smith's application of it to the business firm.[17] If each individual within a factory manufacturing pins goes through all the necessary processes himself, his total daily output will be numbered in tens. If, however, a number of individuals specialize in the different tasks involved (rolling out the metal, hammering it, etc.), the output will be numbered in thousands. The same applies in any type of social endeavour. Too many cooks may spoil the broth, but an assistant to cut up the ingredients to the requisite sizes can be very useful. In the political party, for instance, very little would be accomplished, if every decision had to be taken by all the members in conference. Consequently, there is a specialization which involves some taking a leadership role, and others adopting more passive, if equally essential, roles. Whereas the leadership role involves making decisions, the auxiliary roles will involve the execution of such decisions, propagandizing for their adoption among non-party members and so on.

An individual's *role* within a group or organization is one of the key concepts for the analysis of social or political structures. A role consists of the obligations implicit in an individual's position within the group. That position is itself further defined by the set of rights which the position confers. This distinction can be illustrated by an examination of the academic situation. The role of student involves a series of obligations to imbibe knowledge through attending lectures, reading academic texts and so on. It further involves auxiliary obligations, such as maintaining a semblance of politeness to teachers, not reading newspapers in tutorials and avoiding a degree of dissipation deleterious to serious study. On the other hand, the lecturer's role involves obligations to impart information to the best of his ability, not to slant that information to political purposes and so on. It, moreover, involves auxiliary responsibilities, such as being available to listen to students' study problems, and sometimes even to disentangle their emotional problems to the extent that they impinge on the students' abilities to carry out their work. The student's total position also involves a set of rights. These include the right to adequate tuition, the right to certain financial emoluments under appropriate circumstances and the right to a degree as a reward for the satisfactory performance of his obligations. The lecturer's rights include the freedom to teach what he believes to be true, a reasonable remuneration for his teaching and research activities and some degree of participation in making decisions on the running of the department in which he teaches. If we reserve the term role for the group member's obligations, then that usually given to the rights conferred by his position is *status*. The totality of a member's position within a group, including both obligations and rights, may be termed his *status-role*.

It may be thought that all this is merely a question of terminology and tells us virtually nothing of the dynamics of group structure. In reality, however, the concept of status-role provides an incisive tool for the examination of activities within the group. When we want to look at the workings of groups or organizations, it is rarely that we wish to look at the total human being, but rather we try to isolate only those aspects of his behaviour that are relevant to that particular group context. In other words, we try to define his status-role within that group. The average man is the possessor of many such status-roles, some of which may conflict, and many of which may be quite irrelevant to the analysis of a particular situation. He may be a doctor, a tyrannical father, a cricket club member, but probably only the former will be important for an understanding of his position in the British Medical Association. The dissection of the total human personality involved in assigning him different status-roles in different contexts does not necessarily involve doing violence to the facts of human activity, but mirrors such activity. The whole point about role obligations is that they compartmentalize life, positing different standards of behaviour in different contexts. The Doctor of Medicine has the obligation to cure the sick, and part of that obligation is to refrain from using his position of trust to seduce his female patients. Outside his professional role, however, he may be an incurable womanizer. As long as he does not let such activities interfere with his medical obligations, the B.M.A. and its General Medical Council will be unconcerned. His wife, however, may be concerned, since profligacy of this kind is singularly in conflict with the obligations of a good husband. This example is intended less as a cautionary fable for the medical profession than as an exemplification of the point that each individual has a whole series of status-roles corresponding to the various groups to which he belongs. Another example in a similar vein is provided by the Profumo affair of 1963. Here, there was an almost universal insistence that Profumo's misdemeanour was in lying to the House of Commons rather than in his liaison with the mistress of the Russian naval attaché, and this was surely because the normative obligations of a cabinet minister involve standards of scrupulous honesty, but do not necessarily extend to matters of sexual morality.

It should be very obvious that the concepts of status and role are, except for analytic purposes, inextricably entwined. They are the reverse sides of the same phenomenon. To enjoy the rights implicit in a particular status-role, one must also carry out the obligations it imposes. Indeed, the non-fulfilment of the obligations implicit in a social role almost automatically invoke the most elementary form of social sanction. The doctor who womanizes among his patients rapidly ceases to be a doctor; the group, in this case, the medical profession, debar him from medical practice. The doctor who deceives his wife may cease to be a husband; the community, personified here by the law courts, may debar him from the felicities of married life. Equally, the cabinet minister who lies to the House may be made to resign his position. It should be noted, that in each case the sanction of the removal of the rights implicit in the individual's status-role is accompanied by a degree of moral disapprobation, not merely among the group to which he belonged, but also in the community as a whole. This fact is indicative that even norms specific to a sub-unit of society may be integrated as a general expectation of what conduct is appropriate for group members. Not all members of a society must fulfil the strenuous obligations of a senior politician, but all members of a society expect that cabinet ministers will do so; this is a condition of his receiving the status he does, whether that be measured in terms of financial reward or community respect.

One important conclusion which derives from what has been said to date, is that for every concrete component of society, whether it be the social relationship, the group, or the role-incumbent, there is a complementary normative element. Thus even the simplest sociological formation involves the creation of common expectations of behaviour, the permanent and structured group is regulated by a complex of institutionalized rules and the role-incumbent is directed by the normative content of his status-role. Moreover, it has been argued that for activity to be considered as social it must involve interaction. For a group to have a distinct social existence, rather than mere social significance, there must be interaction among its members, even if this only involves an awareness of, and a dedication to, the common purposes of the group. For instance, a class has a distinct social existence only when its members are aware of their common purposes *vis-à-vis* another class grouping. Where a common situation exists, without such shared purposes, there is merely a potential for action.[18] Groupings without such a common awareness may be described as categoric groups. They include all individuals defined by a common characteristic, but who are unaware of any social signification in their shared situation. All individuals who have red hair constitute a categoric grouping, but, unless they form a pressure group to promote the interests of the red-haired, they cannot be considered to be a social group.[19] A final point, which has already been noted in passing, is that the normative components of social action cannot necessarily be equated with concrete social entities. The norms implicit in social interaction may not be fulfilled under certain circumstances, the incumbent of a particular status-role may not fulfil his normative obligations and the members of a group may diverge from the pattern of activity prescribed by the relevant social institution It is this possible discrepancy between concrete human action and the current normative forms that we describe as conflict or anomie, and it is in the tension that exists when they are present that are found the causes of social change.

Role conflict and reference groups

Attention has so far been largely devoted to the analysis of concepts. This has involved a large degree of concentration on situations approximating to the model of perfect co-operation, since obedience to norms, or the normative patterns involved in status-roles and social institutions, are merely examples of the mechanisms by which social co-operation is maintained. Nonetheless, these concepts have a utility in real situations, in which there is inevitably some admixture of conflict. A neat compartmentalization of the various roles an individual is called upon to play is rarely attainable, and the resulting conflict of obligations may cause uncertainty and confusion. For instance:

> How the expectations of which we are thinking become
> embodied in codes may be illustrated by the dilemma of a
> young woman who became a member of that virile profession,
> engineering. The designer of an airplane is expected to go
> on the maiden flight of the first plane built according to the
> design. He then gives a dinner to the engineers and workmen
> who worked on the new plane. The dinner is naturally a
> stag party. The young woman in question designed a plane.
> Her co-workers urged her not to take the risk—for which,
> presumably, men only are fit—of the maiden voyage. They
> were in effect asking her to be a lady rather than an engineer.
> She chose to be an engineer. She then gave the party and
> paid for it like a man. After food and the first round of
> toasts, she left like a lady.[20]

This situation obviously did not involve too great a role conflict. The individual in question was able to resolve the conflict of her differing obligations involved in the roles of woman and engineer by in part acting out one role and in part the other. Where a conflict is more serious, or more frequently encountered, then normative regulations may develop which legislate on which aspects of which roles may be performed under given circumstances. The relationship between political and business roles in the British context provides a good example of this process. That role conflict can occur, if one man occupies the positions of M.P. or cabinet minister and that of a company director, is obvious. The M.P. or minister may be involved in making decisions from which the individual *qua* company director might derive considerable financial benefit. As the representative of the people, the individual's role obligates him not to divulge information in regard to such decisions or to derive benefit therefrom; as a functionary of the business firm, he has obligations to share-holders and fellow directors to make the maximum possible profit. This dilemma is resolved by the regulations of the House of Commons which state that all M.P.s must declare their financial interests and that ministers must resign their directorships. The reason for this difference in treatment is obvious if one remembers the realities of British government. Backbench M.P.s only discuss policy, whereas ministers make it. Manifestly, the temptation to abuse the role of minister to derive personal benefit is greater than the temptation experienced by the backbencher. Conflicts in status may be similarly used to analyse the position of what has been called the 'marginal' man, the person who does not quite fit in, who feels ambivalent about the society in which he lives. Here, the problems experienced by the Negro professional man in the United States are instructive. The rights which accrue to the professional man, including both remuneration and prestige, are relatively great, but the rights accruing to the Negro are very meagre. His feelings about the society in which he lives are ambivalent because the feelings of others towards him are ambivalent. In the surgery, the patients of the Negro doctor may defer to his opinion as they would to those of any doctor, in the street those same patients may deliberately fail to recognize him.

Conflicts about roles may also occur, not because of an individual having two or more mutually incompatible sets of expectations, but because different individuals may have varying conceptions of a single role. These people we may call his *role-set*. A university lecturer, for instance, has responsibilities to both his students and the university governors. It is in the different conception of the academic's role held by these two bodies that we may seek some of the reasons for student rebellions, that have become such a common phenomenon of campus life. The university authorities may expect the academic to teach skills which fit the student to play a useful role in society. On the other side, the students may expect their mentors to indulge in a radical critique of that society, levelling serious criticisms of the society's social institutions. These two sets of expectations are extremely difficult to reconcile. If the academic does as the authorities desire, the students will regard him as a toady of the Establishment, and if he does as the students desire his employers will probably call him a Bolshevik. This dilemma, and the academic's desire to avoid breaking completely with either set of expectations, is at least one cause of the vast number of wishy-washy 'liberals' to be found in contemporary Senior Common Rooms. To return to politics proper, the same dilemma is manifested in the different conceptions of the politician's role held by his party and his constituents. The former expect him to toe the party line whereas the latter expect him to protect their interests.

An extension of this type of analysis of conflict situations can be made by looking at the individual in relation to the various groups to which he makes reference in patterning his behaviour. Various studies in social psychology have shown just how much the individual's perception of his situation is dependent on group involvement. Sherif describes a dramatic experiment which illustrates this point.[21] Because the circumstances provide no frame of perceptual reference, a stationary point of light in an otherwise completely darkened room appears to dance about. If an individual is put into such a room, he very quickly decides that the light is moving a certain distance, and, having decided on a norm, he will, unless there is outside interference, stick to it. However, if a number of individuals are put in this experimental situation, while their initial estimates of the light's movement will vary considerably, they will soon settle on some norm to which all the individuals composing the group will more or less agree. This is manifestly an example of a group norm arising out of social interaction. The agreement on an arbitrary norm can only be an instance of such social behaviour, since, in reality, the light is not moving at all. A further effect can be observed if into the group is introduced an individual, who is described as an expert on the phenomenon that the group is observing. Let us assume that the group has settled on a figure of three inches as the movement of the light, and that the so-called expert asserts it to be nine inches. Again there will be changes in the group members' perceptions; gradually, their estimates will converge toward the new figure. This occurs because, having accepted the new individual as an expert, they will begin to doubt their former estimates. They will take the expert as a reference point, and so change their perceptions of reality.

The fact that members of a group may take the norms of an outside group as a frame of reference explains much seemingly contradictory social behaviour. The apparently aberrant voting behaviour of the British working class may be regarded, in some part, as an instance of this phenomenon. Trade unionists tend to vote Labour, but non-trade unionists appear to split their allegiances between the Labour and Conservative parties.[22] This may be because some non-trade unionists, in the deferential manner so typical of British politics, take the voting habits of the socially prestigious middle class as worthy of emulation.[23] In other words, these individuals take the middle class as a reference group. This sort of behaviour frequently stems from a desire to achieve the sort of way of life of the reference group members. For instance, the individual who is trying to rise in the world may attempt to ape the habits of those he would become like in order to gain social acceptance. As Merton's discussion of studies carried out on group solidarity within the American army during the last war illustrates, this offers an explanation of the oft-noted phenomenon of 'bucking for promotion'. The private soldier who desires promotion tries to act as he thinks an officer would act; he is bright and alert, he reports breaches of discipline to the N.C.O. and so on. While such behaviour gives him a good chance of promotion, it also makes him thoroughly disliked within the group of which he is currently a member, the group of enlisted men.[24] In other words, reference group activity serves not merely to explain the atypical behaviour of individuals, but also the conflicts within the groups of which they are members.

Moreover, reference group theory may be used to provide a perspective on a further aspect of social behaviour, which is of interest to political studies. As Merton and Kitt suggest, the concept is useful not merely in illuminating behaviour motivated by a desire for upward social mobility, but it may also be utilized to explain the atypical conduct of individuals of high social status, like Karl Marx, who become renegades to their class.[25] Such an individual, although technically belonging to the in-group, has some characteristic which isolates him from it, and this makes him take the in-group as a negative frame of reference. It might be surmised that in Marx's case it was the non-acceptability of his Jewish origin to the bourgeois establishment which made him out of sympathy with the aims of that class.

It should be noted at this point, that it is the individual's social position, as expressed in the complex of roles he performs, that determines his susceptibility to taking the behaviour of other groups as a reference point. This is further illustrated by the differential effect of varying systems of social mobility on reference group behaviour. Where a system of stratification is relatively rigid, as in the Indian caste system, where individuals are assigned a social position in virtue of their birth, it is unlikely that individuals will take the behaviour of higher social ranks as a point of reference. On the other hand, if mobility is greater, and individuals can reasonably expect some improvement in their situation, they are very likely to take higher social strata as models for emulation. This explains one of the paradoxes constantly encountered in analysing comparative political situations. It is not necessarily the poorest who are least satisfied with their lot, but those who have been given some measure of amelioration of their situation, and who have acquired, in consequence, an expectation of still more. In a rigidly stratified system, the poor know that it is their fate to be poor.[26] Where that stratification has broken down, and the individual has the opportunity to improve his life chances to some extent, he begins to compare his situation with those who are still better off. It should be noted that the revolutionary aspirations of the Russian peasant only finally came into the open after the abolition of serfdom. This act gave the peasant some real hope of his condition being improved, but it was a promise which remained unfulfilled. Most of the unstable political situations in the developing countries are unstable despite the fact that the advent of colonialism, and then independence, have improved their material conditions. Prior to the colonial occupation, indeed, they were often highly stable. The problem in these countries is not merely poverty, but more importantly a revolution of rising aspirations. The impact of the West, expressed in colonial occupation and modern technology, has given these nations a reference group by which they may measure their relative impoverishment.

Although in no way exhaustive, the range of examples we have utilized to illustrate the relevance of the concepts of role conflict and reference group to political studies has covered a wide range of social conduct. From voting behaviour to campus discontent, and from the revolutionary impetus of the lone intellectual to the instability of modern nation states, these concepts seem to offer valuable insights for the analysis of political conflict. That these concepts should have such an encompassing range should come as no surprise, since the phenomena to which we have alluded, like all else political, are distinctively social in nature, and so amenable to sociological investigation.

Political socialization

The social and political life of the community is by no means unchanging, but neither is it created anew with each passing generation. Where a social institution defines the purposes of a social group, it achieves a potential immortality and independence of the human frailties of those who compose it. It may lose its existing members, but, assuming there are others willing to subscribe to these purposes, it may continue much as before. This willingness is not, however, primarily a matter of rational choice on the part of the individual, but is rather one of learnt behaviour. Such a learning process, involving the internalization of existing patterns of normative expectations, is called *socialization*, and in the case where these expectations have a political relevance, *political socialization*.

The term socialization is used in preference to learning for a number of reasons. Since what is to be denoted is the process by which individuals assume social roles, it is necessary to differentiate this process from learning which has no such social aspects. For instance, at school we learn many facts about the world in which we live that are irrelevant to the roles we will be called upon to play in later life. Everyone learns that the world is round, but few of us are called upon to use this fact in our everyday tasks. The word socialization, in fact, emphasizes these aspects of learning which are relevant to social life. Moreover the word socialization is used in preference to learning in describing the process of role induction, since the latter word has connotations of a conscious process. Learning is thought of as something that takes place when there is a conscious effort to convey information. But our induction into many roles is by no means a conscious process. The young child is not explicitly taught the social obligations attached to his gender, but, as the Freudian decalogue insists, acquires them in the ordinary course of interaction with his family group. Obviously, this latent process of role learning is most frequently encountered in childhood, and in relation to status-roles within the family, but it also has relevance for political behaviour. It is well known that the Jesuits used to boast that if they had a child in their spiritual care until the age of seven he would always be theirs in spirit. Much the same goes for an individual's political persuasions. Voting studies in Britain and the United States show an extremely high correlation between the voting behaviour of parents and children. This does not occur because parents consciously teach their children to vote Conservative or Labour or Republican or Democratic, but because in the course of childhood and adolescence the individual acquires a whole set of attitudes and opinions which will predispose him to vote as his parents vote.

Although rarely in childhood a conscious process of role learning, socialization at this stage of human development may vary considerably in the degree of explicitness with which it points to adult obligations. The Jesuits of yore did not teach the very young the duty to be of the Catholic faith, since this was assumed, but they taught little else but religious performance. In the Anglo-American political culture, the child is not merely aware of his parents' political attitudes, but very frequently of the party for which they vote. In contrast, the French political culture is much less explicit on this matter. Relatively few interview respondents are able to say with certainty their parents' political persuasion, and it can be argued cogently that this may be a contributory factor in the endemic instability of French voting behaviour.[27]

The efficacy of socialization in the pre-adult stage is partly a concomitant of its unconscious nature. Where a communication is conveyed consciously, it is open to rational acceptance or rejection, but, where the lesson is impressed unconsciously in the course of day-to-day interaction, it becomes an unquestionable verity. The child, unlike the adult, has no fund of experience with which to compare the flow of impressions that his elders, in their wisdom, decide it is suitable for him to receive. Once instilled such impressions are relatively impervious to reality, and the child may find himself as unable as poor Candide to rid himself of the idea 'that in this best of all possible worlds . . . things cannot be other than they are'.[28] The success of childhood socialization is also a result of the child's total dependence on certain adults, particularly his mother and immediate family. His chances of physical survival depend on the care these adults are willing to lavish, and once he is capable of any degree of response these 'significant others' will demand certain performances in return for their attentions. The child's first social obligations are impressed whilst on his mother's knee, and he has practically no alternative but to assume the roles so ascribed. What is learnt in the early period of childhood dependence is rarely of immediate relevance for political behaviour, despite the sometimes mooted suggestion that the 'red tape' mentality is in some way related to the anal stage of personality development. It is of interest, however, that attempts at political conversion in the adult stage very frequently rely on techniques which involve the creation of an artificial situation of childhood dependence. As sociologists have noted, 'brain-washing', the modern refinement of such a conversion technique, is designed to make the individual assume a new role of ideological respectability through the purge of inappropriate social expectations (confession) and the acquisition of new normative patterns (conversion).[29] This is achieved by isolating the individual from the total society, by punishing him and frustrating his normal desires, and then confronting him with an interrogator who, at least, simulates sympathy.[30] To use the terminology of the psychologist, the individual is first reduced to a state of total dependence, and is then confronted by a 'father figure', who is willing to show affection in return for compliance with his expectations. The effectiveness of this technique, while not without its exceptions, is tried and tested, and its success is attributable to placing the victim in a simulated childhood socialization experience.

It has already been pointed out that the degree of explicitness of the political socialization process can affect political behaviour on a cross-national basis, but the same variable may be utilized to explain differences in political orientation as between individuals in the same culture. An example of the way in which an atypical set of childhood influences can determine the choice of the adult role is provided by Harold Wilson, the British Labour Prime Minister.[31] His father was one of the earliest Labour voters and his family in general were involved in political leadership roles. As a small boy, he visited Western Australia and saw his uncle acting as Speaker in the State parliament. Apparently, both he and his parents had decided on a political career from the earliest age. Indeed at the age of eight, he was photographed by his parents on the steps of 10 Downing Street, the Prime Minister's official residence. This type of intense orientation to a given role, which the individual is not yet in a position to assume, is called anticipatory socialization and is akin to reference group behaviour. It gives rise to a situation in which the individual desires to play a role of an out-group member, and in the attempt to succeed in this purpose copies the behaviour appropriate to that role. Like the private soldier 'bucking for promotion', Wilson seemingly took the role of an outside group, the ministerial elite in his case, as that on which to model himself, and apparently all his scholastic achievements were aimed at making him a fitting person to obtain ministerial office. Obviously, the influence of family is not usually so decisive or dramatic, although, one assumes, the family influences on the Prince of Wales are very largely directed to his assumption of the political role of constitutional monarch. In more normal households, however, the individual is subject to a series of latent and manifest socializing influences, which affect his performance of adult political roles. For example, the manner of discipline encountered in the family context may predispose the individual to a more or less authoritarian stance in later life, and there is certainly evidence to suggest:

> An early experience with participation in decision making can increase the child's sense of political competence, provide him with skills for political interaction, and thus enhance the probability of his active participation in the political system when he becomes an adult.[32]

Furthermore, on the more manifest level, the parents' attitudes of respect or scorn for the political system can be inculcated in children in such a way as to influence their later behaviour. It is important to realize that the fact that individuals receive many of their most basic political attitudes from their parents is one of the reasons that political attitudes change so slowly; much more slowly, in fact, than an examination of changes in social and economic structure might lead us to expect. Whereas the government can regulate what is taught in schools, it is very difficult for them to influence the family socialization process. This is one of the reasons it is possible for writers on modern totalitarianism to describe the family as an 'island of separateness'.[33] The family in the Soviet system has not only been known to teach attitudes incompatible with the socialist tenets of the regime, but also to shelter political offenders from the wrath of the law. This instance should not, however, be thought of as a generalization that political socialization acts as a permanent impediment to radical social experimentation. Over a number of decades, the socialist influence may become firmly entrenched, and then political socialization will act as a block to any change away from the prevailing normative pattern. That such changes have already taken place in the Soviet Union is evident. Thus:

> The consensus of observers is that character changes have taken place in the Soviet citizenry since the Revolution . . .

(they) are more overtly disciplined and less spontaneous.
They are more practical and less contemplative; more concerned with results and less with the means whereby they are
gained . . . Regardless of their origin these are traits that
enable men to live and operate more effectively in a modern
industrialized society and particularly in a tightly controlled
system such as the Soviet one.[34]

Apart from the family, the school structure has an important
influence on the growing child. The fact that about twenty-five per
cent of all British Conservative M.P.s went to Eton is an indication
of this.[35] Etonians are chosen, of course, from a select group, whose
family socialization is aimed at fitting them for leadership roles. The
effect of an Eton education is a reinforcement of that socializing
influence. Public schools in general attempt to inculcate the values
appropriate to political leadership, a sense of political rectitude and
a sense of public duty. Such schools are what Goffman calls 'total
institutions', groups which encompass every aspect of the individual's
life whilst he is a member.[36] Because of this, they are able to create
a very similar socialization experience for each child, and so over a
number of years a community of feeling and fellowship. The British
upper classes have similar interests because they have been subject
to a common socializing experience. The prefect system at public
school is one of the devices which create the ability to lead and an
understanding of some of the problems of leadership. In his early
years at school each child is in a position of subservience to his elder
peers who have the power of discipline over him. This does not
create frustration and annoyance for the most part, since each knows
that one day he will have a similar opportunity for control. Although most western school systems avoid taking sides with any
political parties in their teaching, they frequently attempt to create
a more general political loyalty to the community as a whole. Thus
each morning in American schools the children salute the flag.
History lessons, in particular, are oriented to the magnification of
national achievements. To the British, Wellington won the Battle of
Waterloo, but to the German child, it is just as axiomatic that it was
General Blücher. The introduction of African cultural history into
the curriculum of schools in the new states of Africa is meant to
serve the same socializing purpose. Naturally, the school does not
always act as a reinforcing agent. It may, in fact, cross-cut the primary
family influence. The working class boy who attends a grammar
school, which teaches mainly middle class attitudes, and is attended
largely by boys from middle class backgrounds, may at first be
subject to considerable conflict within his role-set. At some point

he may have to make the decision to abandon the values which his family hold dear. Similarly, the middle class adolescent attending university may for the first time in his life meet individuals who criticize the type of society in which he lives. Socialization, whether it be in the context of the family, the school or fully adult groups, is the device by which some degree of social continuity is assured. If the normative patterns, which regulate the functioning of social and political structure, had to be created anew in every generation an ordered existence would be impossible to achieve. As it is, cross-cutting socialization influences and novel experiences uncatered for by learnt normative patterns are conducive to some degree of anomie and conflict in every society. An awareness of the processes by which socialization takes place provides another analytic tool for the explanation of such phenomena.

Conclusion

The political scientist usually comes to his subject-matter, the making of political decisions, with a relatively undeterministic viewpoint. The decision-makers have a choice of alternative courses of action, and political history is the biography of those decisions. Political man, in this view, is a creative being, who shapes the political life in his own image. The sociological approach, which has been offered in these pages, is intended to be a partial corrective to this vision of man unconstrained by the circumstances of his existence. Apart from any biological, psychological and economic constraints which condition political activity, man's ability to make political decisions is constrained by his interaction with others, the roles into which he is socialized and the patterns of morality which his society imposes. To attempt to understand the political life without regard to such factors is to deprive political studies of much of its potential explanatory power. But this assertion should not be taken as denying totally man's ability to shape his world and his social institutions. Institutions change over time because men struggle to make the world more like unto their dreams. Obviously, such individuals are influenced in their actions by their interactions with others, but this does not prevent them from pursuing their aims to the best of their ability. Norms or laws express the conscious or unconscious aspirations of individual men, and other men may one day replace them with other norms and laws more suitable to their situation.[37]

On theory, evidence and insight

The human race, to which so many of my readers belong, has been playing at children's games from the beginning, and will probably do so till the end, which is a nuisance for the few people who grow up. And one of the games to which it is most attached is called, 'Keep to-morrow dark', and which is also named (by the rustics in Shropshire, I have no doubt) 'Cheat the Prophet'. The players listen very carefully and respectfully to all that the clever men have to say about what is to happen in the next generation. The players then wait until all the clever men are dead, and bury them nicely. They then go and do something else. That is all. For a race of simple tastes, however, it is great fun.

The Napoleon of Notting Hill

Irrespective of the nature of the academic discipline one pursues, it is desirable that one has some understanding of the foundations on which that discipline builds its edifice of knowledge. In both political and sociological studies, this question of methodology has aroused a maximum of concern. In comparison with the self-confident natural scientist, who is assured of the validity of his search for the laws which rule the universe, the social scientist is beset by doubts about the possibility of formulating such laws about social conduct, which is the province of his inquiry. In essence, such doubts stem from that creative ability of man to shape the world in the image of his dreams. Man's possession of consciousness, and the ability it gives to manipulate the world of experience, distinguishes him from the dead world of mere matter, and, it can be argued, makes impossible a science of man.

There was never an exact science dealing with individual life. *L'anatomia presuppone il cadavere:* anatomy presupposes a corpse, says D'Annunzio. You can establish an exact science on a corpse, supposing you start with a corpse, but don't try to derive it from a living creature. But upon life itself, or any instance of life, you cannot establish a science . . . There is always the unstable *creative* element present in life, and this science can never tackle. Science is cause-and-effect.[1]

In opposition to this view, we contend that a science of man, comparable with the science of nature, is possible. This contention, which is by no means novel, is not based, however, on the usual assumption that the social sciences can eventually rival the exactitude of the natural sciences. Rather, we would suggest that, in many respects, the methods of the latter are by no means as logically stringent as is frequently opined, and that what the social sciences lose in terms of exactitude may be regained by a superior insight into the nature of the phenomena they study.

The methodology of doubt

On theory

One of the methodologies previously discussed, that of the 'abstracted empiricism' of the behaviouralist school, relies on facticity as a guarantee of the certitude of its knowledge. Such empiricism seeks and discovers truth by accumulating a 'hard' mass of data from which eventually general axioms may be derived. In this view, theory is relegated to the status of an epiphenomenon, an end result, not itself part of the process of scientific discovery. Where 'facts can speak for themselves', the scientific verities are open to the investigator who learns their language, and no doubts need be entertained as to their truth. But if, as we shall argue, all scientific endeavour is fundamentally grounded on theory and generalization, then doubt must be the currency of our provisional acceptance of the world of currently understood scientific knowledge.

As regards the inadequacy of unalloyed empiricism, Andreski points out that: 'It does not require much philosophical sophistication to realize that the mere accumulation of factual data cannot contribute much to our understanding, or even help us decisively in practical action.'[2] Indeed, such an accumulation is inadequate for the purposes of description itself. As Parsons suggests: 'Apart from theoretical conceptualizations there would appear to be no method of selecting among the indefinite number of varying kinds of factual observation which can be made about a concrete phenomenon or field so that the various descriptive statements about it articulate into a coherent whole, which constitutes an "adequate", a "determinate" description.'[3] When it is desired not merely to describe, but to understand the consequences of a given sequence of events, and thus to isolate causal relationships, theory or generalization becomes even more important. It is as true of the natural world as of social life, that 'the available store of interesting and useful information . . . has long ago exceeded the retentive capacity of even the best human mind'[4] and that, in consequence, the only way in which man can acquire an ever greater degree of information about, and consequent control of, his social and natural environment is through the use of general propositions from which deductions about individual cases can be made.

Virtually every action man takes has implicit in it some generalization about the behaviour of physical or social phenomena. To cite two examples:

1 If a man embarks on the perilous adventure of crossing a room, he is, although probably not consciously, relying on certain physical laws about the stress necessary before wooden structures will collapse.

2 If he goes on a, perhaps, hardly less hazardous outing like a political demonstration, and if he is an Englishman, he does so with the implicit knowledge that in the democracy in which he lives policemen rarely turn machine-guns on demonstrators.

On the surface it might be argued that both of these are examples of generalizations that can be made solely on the basis of empirical knowledge already possessed by the actor in question. It might be suggested that, because he had observed a thing in the past, it was likely to continue into the future. But herein enters the element of doubt to which all inductive generalization of this sort, and all theorizing, is subject. Generalizations cannot be made on an empirical basis alone, since it is logically impossible for a set of empirical knowledge to be complete. Even assuming our man did have information about all police provocation in the past, and the circumstances under which it occurred, he cannot have information about all, or indeed any, future instances of such activity. He may be a wise man, but the police may play 'Cheat the Prophet' and use machine-guns the next time around. Generalization from factual information about the past or present is totally dependent on the adequacy of such knowledge, and often it is not such as to provide reasonable grounds for either scientific prediction or human action.

But if into our generalization we introduce a theoretical statement which offers an explanation of the phenomenon in question, we may diminish our degree of doubt, without obviating it entirely. Such a theoretical generalization may be called 'hypothetic' or 'retroductive', and a formal example would be as follows:

1 The surprising fact C is observed.
2 But if A is true, C would follow as a matter of course.
3 Therefore, there is some reason to believe A is true.[5]

What gives this set of propositions coherence, if not logical validity, is statement 2, which is in the form of a theory or a law derived from a theory. To restate our generalization about demonstrations in these terms:

1 The surprising fact is observed that individuals who participate in political demonstrations in England are not machine-gunned by the police.
2 But if it is true that England is a democracy (A democracy pre-supposing non-violent norms for the resolution of conflict), then it would follow as a matter of course that demonstrators would not be machine-gunned by the police.
3 Therefore, there is some reason to believe that England is a democratic country.

In this case, what we know of political demonstrations is being explained by a theory (that England is a democracy), and is being simultaneously used as evidence for a proposition (England is a democratic country). This procedure is patently illogical, but it does reduce our doubt in two ways.[6] First, it does offer a reason for our belief, a frame of reference 'in terms of which empirical scientific work "makes sense" '.[7] It is because Englishmen believe their country to be a democracy that they go on demonstrations without fear. Second, the conclusion, that England is a democracy, is open to test. Other theories might explain the observed phenomenon just as well. For example, the passivity of the police might be explained by the fact that the ruling class was unwilling to show its essentially coercive nature except in circumstances where the rationale of its rule was seriously endangered. A choice between these competing theories can be made, however, by looking at their respective success in explaining other features of the English political system. From each theory inferences or predictions can be drawn, and the more accurate such inferences are 'the less the likelihood of alternative hypotheses which will be adequate to those predictions'.[8]

This methodology of seeking explanation by comparing the predictions derived from theoretical statements with empirical data is general to all scientific endeavour. Einstein's theory of relativity was advanced as making better sense of the data currently known by physics. It was only much later, when exact measurements could be made of the perihelion of Mercury, that the predictions stemming from this theory could be proved to be more accurate than those derived from the Newtonian invariance theory for measure properties. Thus even in physics, the archetypal exact science, it is theory which alters man's conception of the existential universe.

On evidence

To suggest, as we have, that facts cannot speak for themselves, is not to argue that scientific knowledge is not empirically grounded. Empirical knowledge constitutes the evidence in the light of which we grant provisional acceptance to theoretical formulations or reject them. This imbalance between *provisional* acceptance and *outright* rejection is implied in what has already been said about the inadequacy of inductive generalization. To the degree that there is a selection among possible empirical instances, and all past and present instances constitute such a selection, it is possible to find factual confirmation of virtually any hypothesis. By this method, the natural scientist who had spent his entire life on Mount Everest could argue cogently a scientific law that water invariably vaporizes at a temperature below one hundred degrees centigrade. Equally, a Trobriand Island Adam Smith might suggest that economic exchange was, for the most part, a function of the reciprocal offering of gifts.[9] Thus, while it is obvious that many evidential instances are required before a theory may be said to offer even a tentative explanation of reality, no theory can be confirmed definitively on any evidential basis whatsoever.

What can, however, be confirmed is that a particular theory is false. A law derived from theory generates predictions which have an invariant character, and which can ideally be falsified by a single empirical instance. Thus, if our theory postulates that democracy and police violence are incompatible, and we characterize England as a democracy, then a single instance of police violence directed at demonstrators would be sufficient to discount this characterization. In effect, we are suggesting that in place of a false certainty 'deriving from the senses and particulars', we must utilize a methodology of doubt, if we are ever to establish the status of those theories which are our only means of comprehending the existential world. As Karl Popper, the foremost exponent of this view, points out:

> But just because it is our aim to establish theories as well
> as we can, we must test them as severely as we can; that is,

we must try to find fault with them, we must try to falsify
them. Only if we cannot falsify them in spite of our best
efforts can we say they have stood up to severe tests.[10]

Falsification of an invariant statement by a single negative instance is
not quite as simple as it appears. The non-reproducibility of experimental results, the prime criterion of falsification in the natural
sciences, may sometimes stem from the inadvertent neglect of the
ceteris paribus clause, which is integral to all experimental situations.[11]
That extraneous circumstances can prevent one scientist duplicating
another's results is well known, and on the first evidence of falsification the theorist may search around for evidence of such outside
interference, rather than abandon his argument. However, if he fails
to abandon it after subsequent experimental failures have further
sowed the seed of doubt, the academic and scientific community will
abandon it for him.

   In the view here expressed, empirical evidence acquires a scientific
status cognate with the theoretical endeavour. Both are equally
important to the task of promoting our knowledge of the existential
world. Whereas theory suggests explanation in terms of which that
world 'makes sense', empirical evidence discriminates between explanations which are scientific sense and which are nonsense. It is
only when the proponents of either a theoretical or empiricist
approach deny the relevance of each other's work, that they become
the 'Grand Theorists' and 'Abstracted Empiricists' that C. Wright
Mills so rightly decried as destructive of the social sciences, and
science in general.

   The value of empirical scientific work lies in its ability to produce
evidence pertinent to theory, and this is true of all scientific disciplines. But even where this is not denied, it may be suggested that
the sort of evidence that is available to the social sciences is inferior
to that which is offered by those disciplines specializing in the study
of natural phenomena. One such critique of the evidential basis of
the social sciences relates to the very real disparity of measurability
in the different fields. The natural sciences are on the whole amenable
to techniques of precise measurement, whereas, at the moment at
least, this is hardly so of human affairs. The laws of physics, for
instance, tend to be expressed in phrases of great precision, and often
by mathematical formulae, whereas those of sociology and politics
are expressed in terms notoriously open to diverse interpretation.
Partly, this stems from the subject-matter of the social sciences,
which, as Lawrence notes, deal with 'the unstable creative element
present in life'; because no individual in his human uniqueness can
be expressed as a mathematical function, it is suggested that it is

pointless to attempt a scientific study of man. But, insofar as science is a search for explanation which is not falsified by empirical evidence, it only becomes pointless if our techniques for gathering evidence are completely without value. It may be impossible to explain the human uniqueness of man, but as long as there is some aspect of his behaviour which is explicable and unexplained, then the use of a scientific method is both possible and useful.

The relatively brief historical span of the social sciences as explicitly scientific disciplines means that there is no lack of phenomena to be explained. Moreover, various techniques developed by social scientists in recent decades provide means of accumulating evidence for hypotheses regarding human activity. For instance, the impressionistic treatment of historical records can now be supplemented by content analysis of books and documents. This technique, by ascertaining the frequency of certain key-words and phrases, offers a measure of content and impact, which is empirically reproducible by other investigators.[12] Furthermore, the development of survey methods has provided an instrument by which the social scientist is able to extend his investigations into the area of subjective human meaning. What must be subjective meaning to the participant in an interactive relationship can to some degree be regarded as objective information once elicited from that participant. That is to say, once we know someone's views on a subject, we may use this as a datum in predicting his future actions. It was noted previously that for individuals to constitute a class grouping, they must have a common awareness of shared interests or values, and without this characteristic of awareness they could not have an immediate impact on their social and political situation. But it is possible to use survey techniques to find out the degree to which such awareness of class distinction is present in a given population, and such evidence might be utilized for the establishment of theoretical propositions regarding the relationship between self-assigned social class and other behavioural phenomena.

No one would argue that techniques of the kind mentioned are without their problems. There is still a large subjective element present in the procedures utilized to elicit information about opinions, but such procedures are, nonetheless, an improvement on a situation where this sort of information about opinions was altogether unavailable. Furthermore, the very elaboration of empirical procedures which in some way prove inadequate, provide a motive force for the refinement of technique. Thus even a study as much criticized as *The Authoritarian Personality* has led to an awareness of methodological pitfalls to be avoided, such as the danger of results being distorted by the tendency of some individuals to give positive or negative answers to questions irrespective of their content.[13] In the context of measurability, it is also worth mention that increasingly in the social sciences statistical techniques are being used to overcome the problems arising from the seemingly random behaviour of unique individuals. The adoption of this method is not singular to the sciences of man, and it is also an important feature of the study of minute atomic particles and molecular chemistry, in both of which reactions are random, but, let it be stressed, nonetheless predictable.

In any scientific discipline advance may be retarded by the inability to gather the facts which constitute the crucial evidence for current theoretical formulations. It has already been noted that Einstein's theory waited on a technology sufficiently precise to measure the predicted distortion in the perihelion of Mercury. To the degree that such a technology advances so too does our scientific comprehension. As a chronicler of modern developments in the physical sciences suggests:

> The reason why we are on a higher imaginative level is not because we have finer imagination, but because we have better instruments. In science, the most important thing during the last forty years is the advance in instrumental design.[14]

Such advances extend the universe of evidence available for the refutation of our theories, and there is no reason to believe that the advances made in social science technique will be any different in this respect from those made in theoretical physics.

The degree of measurability that can be attained by the social science disciplines is not the only serious ground which can be used for a critique of their evidential basis. As all sociologists have emphasized, man's perception of social facts is a function of the normative expectations and socializing experience to which he has been subject. Man views the social world from the vantage point of a particular status-role, a particular position in the social hierarchy, and that position is likely to influence his evaluation of events which take place in that world. If such evaluations constitute the sole criterion for what we designate as evidence, then there will be as many social sciences as there are societies with disparate normative patterns.

While the most extreme version of this argument is paradoxical, in that the assertion that all knowledge is relative to the assertor's social position must be equally applicable to the proposition just advanced, there is no doubt that social position can affect evidential judgment. The problem which then arises is whether the extent of this distortion is such as to make impossible an empirical science of man. Certainly social scientists, whether they inhabit academic ivory towers or are practical men of affairs, do not act as if they believed this to be true. Like the engineer, who uses his factual knowledge of the structural stress of building materials to design a building which will not collapse, the authors of the Beveridge Report used their knowledge of social and economic conditions in Britain in order to design a welfare system which would eliminate poverty and the most blatant elements of social inequality. The recent tendency for new states to invite eminent political scientists to write their constitutions similarly involves a commitment to the idea that political scientists have a fund of factual knowledge which will be efficacious in designing new political institutions. Despite the Marxists' avowed distain for such 'social engineering', it is notable that the succession of Russian Five Year Plans constitute probably the most ambitious attempt to utilize economic information to the end of the conscious manipulation of the social environment.

The reason that social scientists can take this stance of assuming their knowledge to have pertinence to the problems of the real world is that their knowledge can be tested by evidential reference to the real world. All the examples given above consist of implicit theoretical statements, predictions drawn from them and delineations of the evidence that would be required to falsify those predictions. The political scientist who recommends a federal constitution for a state in which tribal animosities are firmly entrenched works on the basis of an implicit theory that the centrifugal forces inherent in tribalism can only be attached to a national concept of legitimacy if some formal recognition is given to separate tribal identity. The prediction that separate parliaments for separate tribal areas will obviate the violent rending of the political structure by these centrifugal forces is based on evidence derived from knowledge of other federal systems and is falsifiable in terms of evidence that will be supplied by the future conduct of the tribal society for which he writes a constitution. The possibility of falsification is the crucial element in this process, for having asserted the precise consequences of a theory, the social scientist is in a position to be contradicted by all men irrespective of their normative frame of reference.

This is as true of the other examples given, although it might be postulated that the effacement of poverty was a question of evaluation, since poverty is itself a valuational concept. Certainly, socialists and conservatives are likely to disagree on what constitutes a state of poverty, but there is no reason why social scientists need be a party to such disagreements. As modern linguistic philosophy insists, words are merely tools which we use in communicating ideas, and these ideas should have meanings which it is possible to operationalize. Laymen may disagree about the nature of poverty, but the social scientist should make explicit his use of the term. Modern surveys of the phenomenon of poverty have drawn a poverty line expressed in money terms, and in those terms it is possible for all men to judge whether a given method of social amelioration achieves the objective of eliminating poverty.

Like so much of the scientific endeavour, our limited confidence in the evidential basis of a science of man rests on a methodology of doubt. It is only when doubt is impossible that science becomes untenable. The belief that there is a life after death is unfalsifiable, and, while that belief may be correct, it can never become a province of scientific investigation. As long as assertions about social and political life are open to doubt, there remains scope for a social and political science.

The methodology of faith

> The microbe is so very small
> You cannot make him out at all,
> But many sanguine people hope
> To see him through a microscope.
> His jointed tongue which lies beneath
> A hundred curious rows of teeth;
> His seven tufted tails with lots
> Of lovely pink and purple spots . . .
> All these have never yet been seen—
> But scientists, who ought to know,
> Assure us that they must be so.
> Oh! Let us never, never doubt
> What nobody is sure about!
>
> *More Beasts For Worse Children*

On insight

The methodological canon of testability, that which we have called the methodology of doubt, is possibly the most misunderstood aspect of the social sciences' conceptual armoury. At their most extreme, the proponents of this doctrine have suggested that this criterion serves to distinguish scientific knowledge from metaphysics, not knowledge from illusion, or truth from falsity. Indeed, Karl Popper is willing to defend non-empirical statements, or metaphysics, not merely because they often serve as a psychological impetus to scientific imagination and insight, but because they may occasionally be actually conducive to the elaboration of scientific theory.[15] This would certainly appear to have been the case of Maupertius, the eighteenth-century mathematician, whose development of the Newtonian laws of motion 'started with the idea that the whole path of a material particle between any limits of time must achieve some perfection worthy of the providence of God'.[16] The basic point that is stressed by Popper is the difference in logical status of the manner in which we accept the truth or falsity of statements, and the manner in which we arrive at such statements. Certain models like that of the harmony of the spheres or the survival of the fittest may themselves be entirely unamenable to falsification, and consequently be 'unscientific' in Popper's usage, but yet be generative of statements which can be tested.[17]

Indeed Popper's restriction of the word 'scientific' to those statements capable of falsification may in itself be regarded as not a little tendentious, since it excludes much of the insight and analogy that is essential to the process of scientific discovery. It is indubitable that empirical testing is a necessary condition of scientific achievement, but whether it is a sufficient one is less certain. The convictions on which much of the theorizing in modern physics rests seem little less dubious than those entertained by Maupertius. For instance, Einstein's and others' rejection of the principle of indeterminacy seems to stem from an unwillingness to 'believe that God plays with dice'.[18] Such an insight as this is not per se 'unscientific', it is rather that its full scientific value cannot be realized unless it is elaborated in such a way that it becomes amenable to testing. Much the same can be said for those conceptual schemata or metatheories which are so frequently criticized in the social science context. Marx may not have been accurate, for instance, in his claim that his theory constituted 'scientific socialism', since so much of his argument is incapable of falsification, but to dismiss his insights into the causal nexus between economic and social structure on this ground alone constitutes something akin to charlatanism. Quite apart from the fact that the modern discipline of economic history is based precisely on that insight, the only way in which Marx's view could be rejected as scientifically worthless would be if all attempts to operationalize and falsify it were unsuccessful.

Virtually all the founding fathers of the discipline of sociology believed in the need for insights prior to investigation, which of their very nature must be untestable. This is certainly true of both Durkheim and Weber. As the former suggested:

> It is a vain delusion to believe that the best way to prepare for the advent of a science is first to accumulate patiently all the materials it will use, for one can know what these needed

materials are only if there is already some presentiment of its essence and its needs.[19]

Such a presentiment was also what Weber sought in elaborating his methodology of ideal types. Only through a 'one-sided accentuation' of features of the concrete situation was it possible to acquire an insight into the relationships of the *dramatis personae* of the social stage. As he suggested, such ideal types may serve 'as a harbour until one has learned to navigate safely in the vast sea of empirical facts'.[20] Neither Weber nor Durkheim believed that a science of society should eschew the testing of theory by appeal to empirical data, but both argued forcibly that such testing did not alone constitute social understanding.

That metatheoretical models, and other untestable 'noble abstractions', constitute a major source of scientific and particularly theoretical, insight has two important implications. First, alongside the methodology of doubt we must be willing to embrace a methodology of faith, at least in respect of the process of scientific discovery. The analogy from which insight stems is an argument that the relationship we are attempting to explain works like something else, but what else we cannot know until the discovery has been made. Consequently, we must have faith in insights, from whatever source they come, to the extent that they give even a promise of deepening our understanding of the world. The function of insight is to shed light where formerly there was darkness, but such illumination is not necessarily of a kind that empiricism can admit into its pantheon. Second, we must not ask of metatheory what we ask of scientific theory. By definition, the possibility of falsification which is the major criterion of scientific theory is missing in metatheory. As we shall subsequently argue, one of the most tragic confusions of the contemporary social sciences lies in the assertion of those who advance metatheories that they are in fact scientific explanations of the existential world, and the complementary rejection of metatheoretical formulations by critics who argue that they are incapable of empirical refutation. The tasks of scientific theory and metatheory are different, and only if they are judged in respect of their success in carrying out their different functions can they both contribute to the furtherance of our knowledge.

On social reality and literature

While the two methodologies of doubt and faith are common to both the natural and social sciences, the range of insights available to each will tend to vary. The sort of insight which is illuminating in the social and political context is not necessarily useful in the study of inanimate nature, and *vice versa*. The concluding section of this chapter attempts to show some of the sources of insight which are peculiar to the study of man.

Perhaps the greatest appeal of the methodological canon of testability by reference to observational data lies in its supposed emphasis on reality. In demonstrating the validity of an argument it is essential that the evidence evinced be reproducible in order to convince even the most sceptical of the relevant community of scholars. This methodological necessity, however, is sometimes interpreted to imply that the only data which can promote our understanding of social processes is of the kind provided by modern survey techniques. Demonstrably, such an assumption is not required by the canon of testability. What is demanded is observation, not a particular technique of observation. To argue the contrary is to maintain that an understanding of society is only as old as the invention of the interviewer's clip-board.[21] The utility of such techniques for the testing of certain hypotheses is indisputable and, as Merton has noted, they may occasionally, when their results are unanticipated, strategic, and anomalous, serve to shape the development of theory.[22] On the other hand, research data acquired in this way are by no means the only type of information we possess which may be pertinent for theoretical purposes. Most particularly we possess information about the nature of social processes in virtue of our nature as social beings. Indeed, as Percy Cohen has pointed out:

> By participating in social life men have a far greater chance of comprehending certain features of its fundamental reality, than they do by participating in the natural world. The fact that men are physical objects does not give them access to the nature of matter or life. The fact that men are social subjects, as well as objects, does give them the opportunity to gain some idea of the nature of social relationships and of the wider context of these. For social reality does not have mechanisms which are *necessarily* hidden from the observation of all those who participate in it.[23]

In other words, although the social scientist may quite frequently be unable to emulate the physicist in quantifying his observations, he has the advantage of some degree of empathy with his material, which the natural scientist can only achieve in the most indirect fashion; by, in Dirac's words, seeking to achieve 'beauty in one's equations'.[24] By relying solely on the type of observational material provided by the survey technique the social scientist disavows his only advantage. This disavowal reaches the proportions of an abdication of responsibility when it is carried through to teaching. The student is not just an empty slate on which can be inscribed the 'golden rules' of falsifiability and random sampling; rather he is a social and political animal, who, although he may never have consciously reflected on it, has a wide experience of social relationships. The task of the social scientist *qua* teacher is consequently to make the student overtly understand and evaluate what he has previously unreflectively experienced. The student comes to his subject with a vast mass of unanticipated, strategic and anomalous material pertinent to the explanation of social processes, and it should be the object of instruction continuously to recreate the serendipity pattern. In part this means the learning of methods of rational proof and observation, but it also means resorting to the experiences of others who have attempted to interpret similar phenomena. This does not merely imply going to the founding fathers of the social science disciplines, but to all those who have tried to express and understand the human condition. Particularly, it means going to literature, since, without any demands being made for falsifiability, the great playwrights, novelists, and poets have been attempting to comprehend the nature of social relationships for millennia before the idea of social science was born. It is not for nothing that Popper calls what has come to be known as the 'self-fulfilling prophecy', the 'Oedipus effect'. Almost five hundred years before Christ, Sophocles graphically illustrated in the story of *King Oedipus* the tragic way in which prophecy could interfere with human destiny.

It is certainly the case that many of the insights achieved by social scientists this century have been a rediscovery of truths told men by bards of past epochs. This does not mean, of course, that the social sciences have achieved nothing. As Lewis Coser has pointed out: 'fiction is not a substitute for systematically accumulated knowledge'.[25] Like all acts of reflective understanding, the insights it can provide have only a subjective certitude, and will almost invariably be vulnerable in the sense that many questions on the same issue have yet to be asked.[26] It is in devising a methodology of empirical testing which can provide some degree of objective certitude, and in reducing the vulnerability of social insights by systematic investigation of related hypotheses, that the social sciences have shown their greatest achievement. But despite the need to test and circumscribe the insights we acquire through participation in, or empathetic observation of, social reality, it is nonetheless apparent that we ignore the insights and suggestions of literature at our peril. Even a few examples will illustrate this point. It might be expected that any contemporary departure in social and political relationships would be fully chronicled by the social scientist long before it became the received wisdom of literature. However, the theory of mass society utilized by modern political theorists as an explanation of the rise of totalitarian regimes was predated by many novels which examined the theme of man's rootlessness in modern industrial society and his consequent urge to accept messianic political leadership. Franz Kafka, at least implicitly, illustrates the manner in which the ethos of bureaucratic organization may be conducive to this result. The trial of modern man is the inexorable quality of the rules by which he lives and their commensurate incomprehensibility.

Even the heuristic devices of some social scientists have already been quite explicitly utilized by the writers of fiction. What Lermontov says of his own novel is surely only a premonition of the ideal type: 'A Hero of Our Time, gentlemen, is in fact a portrait but not of an individual; it is an aggregate of the vices of our whole generation in their fullest expression.' That such historical constructs should be found in literature is perhaps not surprising, but that generalized explanatory model of social relationships, which Robert Bierstadt considers the hall-mark of sociological thinking, is itself by no means absent.[27] Indeed to Martin Esslin, the characteristic which gives to Ibsen's play, *An Enemy of The People*, its enduring quality is precisely the manner in which he captures those political relationships which are not localized in time and space.

> The struggle for power, for the support of the majority in one form or another, these were the essence of politics then as they are now and as they have been in any other historical epoch. Always the politicians have been involved in the dilemma that to retain their power and influence they must serve the sectional interests of their supporters, even if they can clearly discern the long-term advantage of short-term sacrifices on their part . . . The clarity of the vision, the economy of the technique with which Ibsen has succeeded in compressing these eternal elements of all politics into the compass of a small, compact community, of a single dramatic conflict, is a truly astonishing proof of his genius.[28]

Perhaps best of all, Fielding recognizes the dangers of making certain types of unfalsifiable assertion. The presumption that an individual has a particular interest is compatible with very diverse manifestations of activity. Thus:

> Nay, the more civility she showed him, the more they conceived she detested him, and the surer schemes she was laying for his ruin; for as they thought it her interest to hate him, it was very difficult to persuade them she did not.[29]

This insight about the nature of interest analysis is one which a number of contemporary pressure group theorists might well take to heart.

Even these few examples may illustrate that literature is not without relevance to the study of social and political reality. The sometimes suggested distinction between the Two Cultures is in the case of the social sciences at least a dangerous one. Our scientific knowledge will never be so firmly grounded that we can despise the heritage of social insight with which the humanities can provide us. As our introductory chapter on sociology and the discipline of politics suggested, a similar case can be argued for the relevance of insights from one social science discipline to another. The explicit premise of this book is that political studies can gain from insights derived from the wider culture of sociology, and the remaining chapters explore the insights offered by some of the most important sociological metatheories.

Functionalism as metatheory

Metatheory, analytical theory, noble abstraction, conceptual model or scheme are all words which sociologists have used to refer to those speculations which, while themselves untestable by reference to evidential criteria, serve to point to the type of causal factors which might be appropriate for the explanation of a given situation. The types of metatheory that can be used to interpret social reality are many and various. Inkeles, for instance, lists the following kinds of model that are used in sociology: the evolutionary model, which sees society 'progressing up definite steps of evolution leading through even greater complexity to some final stage of perfection'; the organismic model, which sees society as being similar in nature to an organism; the conflict model, of which Marxism is a variant, and which sees society as being torn by omnipresent conflict; the physical science model and various types of mathematical model.[1] To these might be added the machine model[2] and the cybernetic model, the latter of which sees society as working in a similar manner to the communications system in the human brain or computer.[3] Partly cross-cutting these types of conceptual model is perhaps a more basic division of metatheoretical approaches. This division is between approaches that see the basic fact of social living as the stability of equilibrium of the social fabric, and those which see it rent apart by constant strife. Structural-functionalism, whose original insight owed much to organic analogy, sees social solidarity as the important category of social explanation, as in a way do the various evolutionary models. On the other side are those who feel that conflict between individuals and groups is the stuff of society and politics, and that our understanding of these realms can only be furthered by understanding social conflict. In recent decades, this simple division of approach has been complicated by those who feel that the most salient fact of modern living is neither stability nor conflict, but the incomprehension of most people of the demands made on them by leaders and social organizations. This then constitutes a third basic approach; that of anomie or the theory of mass society. It will be apparent that these three basic metatheoretical approaches are analogous of the three types in which the simplest sociological formation is manifested, which we termed perfect co-operation, perfect conflict and perfect anomie. This should not be in the least surprising. It is merely to say that the metatheoretician who talks about social stability is emphasizing those social interactions which nearest approach perfect co-operation. Similarly, he who emphasizes social dissensus depicts the world as one based on perfect conflict, and he who points to the manipulated aimlessness of modern man sees in everything perfect anomie.

This brings us to a final point before embarking on an analysis of the structural-functional model. In discussing the nature of the three basic forms of social interaction it was argued that they were never found in pure form. It was suggested that there was never a relationship, much less a society, in which co-operation was maintained without any friction and, contrariwise, it was noted that a relationship based on perfect conflict or anomie was a contradiction in terms. This immediately implies the conclusion that no single metatheoretical formulation will be adequate to provide explanations for all of social reality. This marks another difference between scientific theory and metatheory, for while two scientific theories offering different predictions cannot both be correct, different, and indeed contradictory, metatheories can simultaneously illuminate the nature of social reality. We would in fact suggest the tentative conclusion, to which we shall later return, that the metatheoretical models we shall examine are complementary, and that only through a willingness to use them all can the social or political scientist hope to explain the full range of the phenomena that confronts him.

Functionalism and the analysis of systems

Structural-functional analysis has in recent years become a rather popular device for the analysis of political situations. In order to introduce the topic, we will give two examples of its use in such a context.

1 Boss politics The first of these is provided by Merton's classic discussion of the latent functions fulfilled by the American political machine.[4] The usual view of the machine boss is that he is part of a corrupt institution by which political parties gain votes in return for favours received. In American political history, there have been numerous attempts to extirpate the machine boss in the name of 'good government'. Merton's analysis of bossism, however, points to a series of functions the boss carries out for diverse groups in the community. To see machine politics as a moral evil without realizing that it serves the latent or manifest needs of individuals is, he argues, not merely inaccurate, but inconducive to the social engineering required for removing the more corrupt aspects of the institution. His basic case is as follows. The United States constitution was designed by its architects to obviate the possibility of any individual's acquiring highly centralized power. By the institution of a system of checks and balances, it was hoped to create a situation in which no one could accrue sufficient power to endanger liberty. This kind of institutional arrangement, however, tends to discourage the growth of effective and responsible leadership. If any individual wishes to procure a decision favourable to his interests, he has to go through a long and complicated procedure. He has to persuade not merely one group of leaders, as in Britain, where the Cabinet has ultimate jurisdiction of all authoritative decisions, but State governments, Federal government, Congress and President. Merton's point is that the structure of government in the United States is not favourable to procuring rapid satisfaction of community interests. This being so, the political machine arose as an alternative structure which is capable of carrying out this function of procuring authoritative decisions.

At least four major community groupings can be identified which satisfy their demands through the institution of the political boss. The political machine satisfies social welfare needs. One of its strengths lies in the fact that it has roots in the local community and neighbourhood. Because the individual feels he has a personal relationship with the precinct captain, he will go to him in times of trouble. The machine frequently provides food for those in poverty, jobs for those who need them and it may even award a political scholarship to the poor boy who is without the means to attend college. The client of the political machine may well prefer to ask for aid from the personally known machine boss, rather than rely on the bureaucratic social welfare apparatus. Moreover, the machine also serves the function of providing favours to local businessmen. As Merton notes:

> Business corporations, among which the public utilities
> (railroad, local transportation and electric light companies,
> communications corporations) are simply the most

conspicuous in this regard, seek special dispensations which will enable them to stabilize their situation and to near their objective in maximizing profits.[5]

The machine boss is in a perfect position to carry out this function with a minimum of inefficiency, since he holds the strings of diverse governmental divisions, bureaux and agencies, and is thus able to rationalize relations between the government and private enterprise.

This function is obviously one of the reasons why the political machine has acquired a reputation for corruption. Another even more obvious cause lies in the fact that the machine often carries out similar services for illicit business, the racketeers and shysters. Leaving aside considerations of morality, rackets, vice and crime are just like legal businesses insofar as they need to make a profit, and in consequence demand favourable decisions from the government. Most particularly, they desire the very minimum of government intervention in their affairs, and in return for such protection they provide funds for the party machine. Lastly, the machine serves the function of offering a channel of social mobility for disadvantaged sections of the community. The political control of the machine acquired by immigrant populations has given them a foothold on the ladder to social advancement that would otherwise have been absent.

2 *Political systems* A second, and very different, example of the functionalist analysis of political life is offered by Almond's discussion of 'A Developmental Approach To Political Systems.'[6] In this article, Almond suggests that we may visualize the political activities of a society as a system marked off from its environment by boundaries. The distinction between political system and environment is postulated by the following definition:

> The political system is that system of interactions to be found in all independent societies which performs the functions of integration and adaptation by means of employment, or threat of employment, of more or less legitimate compulsion.[7]

Every social and non-social aspect of life which falls outside the arena of the use of more or less legitimate compulsion consequently constitutes part of the political system's environment. In terms of this kind of model, the functions isolated are necessarily a concomitant of the need to relate system and environment. There are *input* functions which are concerned with the way in which the environment affects the political system; there are *output* functions which are concerned with the impact of the political system on the environment, and there are *conversion* functions which deal with the internal task of the political system of converting inputs into outputs.

Two types of input function can be postulated. Individuals in their non-political roles may make various demands of the political system. Among these, the most usually emphasized is the demand for goods and services. Very frequently individuals judge those in full-time political roles by whether they can literally 'bring home the bacon'. Other demands relate to the regulation of behaviour. As political philosophers have often emphasized, the function of government is not merely to provide prosperity, but an ordered state, in which life is not 'poor, nasty, brutish and short'. Further demands may relate to symbolic inputs, which in this day and age usually relate to symbols of national pride, and to participatory inputs, demand for a greater involvement in political decision-making. But individuals do not merely make demands of the political system; they also offer it support of various kinds. These support functions include material willingness to provide the resources necessary to service the political system, obedience to laws and customs, participation in the political process and manifestations of deference to authority.

The task of the political system is to convert these inputs into authoritative decisions or outputs. These output functions include the allocation and distribution of goods. The vast importance of this function can be gauged by the high percentage of national income which is distributed by the public sector in all advanced economies. A complementary function relates to the enactment of tax or tribute systems which meet this burden of public expenditure. Furthermore, political systems provide an output of regulations of behaviour and symbolic affirmations of values. They wave the flag and brandish the policeman's baton.

The functions involved in converting inputs to outputs require certain performances on the part of political role players. There must be some provision for the communication of demands, and in modern politics this *political communication* function is increasingly taken over by the mass media. Individuals must be recruited into political roles, and, as we have seen, this *political socialization* task is largely carried out by the agencies of family and school. Other functions include *interest articulation*, a process by which demands can be made explicit, and *interest aggregation*, which involves the transformation of articulated demands into wider and more coherent policy proposals. Lastly, there is a series of tasks involved in the governing process itself. Mechanisms are necessary for the conversion of policy alternatives into authoritative decisions (*rule making*), for the application of general rules to particular cases (*rule application*) and for the adjudication of rules in individual cases (*rule adjudication*).

Despite the great differences between the two examples cited, they do have one element in common. Both focus on what political actors do, the functions they perform, rather than on the structures which perform them. Crudely put, Merton's argument is that individuals desire the performance of certain functions, and, in the absence of governmental agencies which are capable of carrying them out, they will accord some degree of support to alternative structures which do have that ability. In Almond's model, there is, indeed, a conscious attempt to get away from structural categories and to concentrate on the tasks of the political system. Rather than use terms with structural connotations, like government, executive and judiciary, he offers ones which have only a performance aspect, like rule making, rule application and rule adjudication. The functionalist takes function as an independent variable and structure as a dependent one, because, for a given social situation, the tasks which individuals demand to be performed are invariant, while the structural arrangements available for the tasks are many in number.

The major distinction between the two examples lies in their differential amenability to empirical testing. It is manifest that the developmental approach to political systems is an almost pure instance of metatheory. This picture of the political system and its environment provides us with a set of conceptual categories, which, it may be suggested, are relevant for the understanding of all concrete politics. Rather than offering any kind of explanation in itself, it offers a check-list of questions that the political scientist would be advised to ask. Thus in interpreting the real political situation of the Weimar Republic in the 1920s, we might be led to ask questions about the regime's capabilities for producing outputs. In this context, it might be suggested that the reparations policy of the Allies prevented the authorities from converting demands for material satisfactions into realizations of such demands. Again, it might be noted that group animosities were so great that no output of symbols could satisfy everybody. A nation's flag is a very potent symbol of national unity, but the Weimar flag could satisfy neither the Communists' desire for the red flag of workers' solidarity, nor the traditionalist demands for the red, gold and black flag of the Reich. These answers do not constitute a scientific explanation of the fall of the Weimar Republic, because the degree of output capacity that a political system must achieve is not specified in terms amenable to evidential falsification. There is no reason to believe that such a specification will never be attainable, particularly in the form of probabilistic statements of the impact of function performance, but, even it were, the scientific status of such specifications does not imply a similar status for the questions from which such specifications are derived.[8] A model of the kind proffered by Almond does not explain anything, but rather suggests lines of investigation and explanation, and its usefulness is to be judged by the extent to which political scientists find its conceptualization illuminating.

The Mertonian discussion is quite different in that it does suggest an explanation of machine politics. The argument constitutes an explanation simply because it is in theory capable of refutation. Regarded merely as a description of the functions performed by the political machine, it could be falsified by evidence that the suggested benefits accruing to community groupings from its existence were not in fact realized. Regarded as a theoretical formulation, the argument can be utilized to generate predictions capable of evidential testing. For instance, it might be postulated that in any polity in which governmental procedures were not favourable to the rapid satisfaction of community interests, there would arise more or less corrupt structures for the performance of this function. While it is not our intention to do more than argue that the Mertonian explanation is capable of falsification, it might be noted that the corruption of civil servants in the developing countries does seem to provide favourable evidence for this hypothesis, as does the institution of Tolkatchi, or procurers of scarce industrial goods, in the Soviet economic system.[9] This contrast of examples illustrates once again the point that in any concrete orientation to the study of society, there will be encountered elements of scientific theory and metatheory masquerading under the same title. This is of no great import to the degree that we are capable of differentiating them when the need arises. It is, however, the case that much of the dispute and controversy about the methods and logic of functional analysis arise from an inability to make this distinction.

The logic of functional analysis

This coalescence of theory and metatheory under a single rubric stems from the functionalist's definition of the subject-matter of his studies in a manner which stresses the common element in both. In this delineation, functionalism becomes a method of relating individual actions to their wider consequences in terms of the functions, latent or manifest, which they carry out. It will be immediately apparent that such a formulation leads in its metatheoretical variant to an emphasis on stability and co-operative activities. The type of questions that we are prompted to ask are of the kind which ask how individuals and groups by their actions contribute to the maintenance of existing structures. It is a functionalist metatheory, which makes Merton take the novel approach of asking not why the political machine is corrupt, but what it does to satisfy the demands of diverse social groupings. Certainly, the conceptual categories of Almond's functional model are delineated in such a way as to emphasize political stability. The functions outlined are not themselves neutral, the effective performance of which lead to stability, the ineffective performance to instability. Rather it is assumed that performance as such means stability, and non-performance, instability. Although there is no logical reason why it should be so, it is often assumed that the performance of functions is *per se* desirable, and their non-performance undesirable. In the developing countries, for instance, the articulation of interests is less manifest than in the West, and since this tends to be associated with a high degree of political instability, which the western political scientist deprecates, there is a considerable tendency for a negative value-judgment to enter into the discussion. This emphasis of functionalist metatheory on stability does not, however, logically preclude such analysis from illuminating processes of social change. Nor is it exclusively an ideology of the status quo, as some of its critics maintain, but, as we shall see, it is in these areas that its emphasis on co-operation tends to obscure social reality to some degree.

Historically, the origin of the functionalist model may be found in the reaction against the school of conjectural history among social anthropologists in the early part of the century. This latter school attempted to explain the institutions of primitive societies as survivals of older forms of social organization. For instance, they came to the fallacious, or rather untestable, conclusion that such primitive customs as religious prostitution and festive licence, which are the rule in most simple forms of society, were survivals of a universal primitive promiscuity.[10] This kind of argument hardly constitutes an explanation, since it explains existing customs by reference to an imaginary previous social organization for which no empirical evidence, other than the current customs, exists. At its inception, functionalist theory rested on an organic analogy drawn from the biological and physiological sciences. In perhaps its most extreme form, this took the shape of a societal structure based on the individual's biological needs. Other early proponents of the perspective, like Durkheim, saw society as being a structure designed to meet societal needs in much the same way as physiological processes met the needs of the organism. Rather than analyse primitive customs in terms of conjectural history, these early functionalists saw:

... the family, the clan, sexual restrictions, as well as sexual liberties ... not as stages of a transformation nor fortuitous indices of cultural type or cultural stratum, but correlated, component parts of one big institution; the institution which controls the mating of sexes, the procreation of offspring and the education of the young, and fulfils the integral function of racial and cultural continuity.[11]

Perhaps the basic perspective inherent in functionalism can be made clearer by outlining how one of its most famous exponents came to adopt it. Talcott Parsons starts his functionalist analysis by asking how the Hobbesian problem of order is solved in existing societies. Hobbes' argument was that individuals are naturally antagonistic, and, unless a sovereign with unlimited power is instituted by their joint agreement, the only conceivable result is 'the war of all against all'. Since it is evident that at least some elements of stability are manifested by social structure, Parsons suggests that there must be some societal arrangements which mitigate the disruptive effects of the clash of individual interests. These arrangements may be visualized as functions necessary to societal preservation.[12] This view can be formalized by drawing up a list of functions which must be fulfilled by any society in order for it to survive as a self-sufficient system of action. Such a list might include the maintenance of an adequate relationship with the environment, sexual reproduction, role differentiation, role assignment and shared cognitive orientation.[13] Obviously, no society can exist where individuals are unable to procure material satisfactions from their environment, where provision is not made for the recruitment of new role-players from within the social structure (consequently, a monastery cannot be regarded as a society in this sense, although there are reasons for believing that the First Estate might have had some claim to this status), and the point about shared cognitive orientations is only to repeat our previous argument, that unless individuals have some shared expectations the formation of social relationships is impossible. The examination of the functions which a society must carry out is a preliminary to an examination of the structures through which these functions are articulated, and it is this relationship between structure and function which constitutes the central perspective of the theory. The metatheoretical orientation to stability can be seen in the emphasis on those elements of social reality which promote the survival and maintenance of the on-going social system.

The later history of functionalism has to some degree been one of the abandonment of the more extreme corollaries of the organic analogy, and it is in this form that it has been largely used in modern political analysis. The use of analogy cannot be condemned as such.

The methodology of faith consists of the search for conceptual analogies of processes which are currently opaque and incomprehensible. The fact that society is not an organism does not mean that it is not illuminating to look at social processes as if they were analogous to physiological processes, and, indeed, the virtue of metatheoretical insights lies in the ability they confer to look at social behaviour in terms of a worked-out and tested framework of ideas. Analogy only becomes a stumbling-block to knowledge when it is stretched too far. In this context, the early functionalists made at least three assumptions, largely based on their organic analogy, which, as Merton has pointed out, are extremely dubious, and inconducive to the eventual generation of testable hypotheses.[14]

1 The assumption of *functional unity*, which posits that standardized social activity or cultural items are functional for the entire social system. Malinowski's contention that 'belief and ritual work for social integration, technical and economic efficiency, for culture as a whole—indirectly therefore for the biological and mental welfare of each individual member' is an example of such an assumption.[15] Such a contention is challenged by the manifest fact that certain social activities are blatantly harmful to certain groups within a society. Slavery may, for instance, be functional for the preservation of a privileged class, but hardly from the point of view of the slave. The assumption must be replaced by the specification of what units are served by the performance of the function, and the additional concept of *dysfunction*, which covers these instances when social activities impede the purposes of a given unit.

2 The early functionalists tended to assume a *universal functionalism*, which posited that all social and cultural items fulfil sociological functions. This view was intended as a challenge to the idea of cultural survivals existing for no apparent social purpose. The assumption is, of course, totally unfalsifiable, and is not, for that matter, a correct application of the organic analogy. By no means all parts of the organism perform functions designed to promote organic survival. Merton suggests that in place of this assumption, it would be more reasonable to postulate that:

> . . . persisting cultural forms have a net balance of functional
> consequences either for society considered as a unit or for
> sub-groups sufficiently powerful to retain these forms intact,
> by means of direct coercion or indirect persuasion.[16]

This weakened version of the functionalist statement would cover the Marxist view that religion is an 'opiate of the masses' which functions to preserve the economic interests of the ruling class by attenuating claims for equality in this life.

3 The assumption of *functional indispensability*, which postulates that all social and cultural items are indispensable. As Hempel notes, this assumption makes the error of elevating the logical fallacy of affirming the consequent into a basic principle of sociological theory. Such an explanation has the following form:

> 1. At a given time (T), a system (S) functions adequately in a specified setting (C).
> 2. S functions adequately under conditions (C) only if certain necessary conditions (N) are satisfied.
> 3. A given trait (I) would, if present in S, satisfy conditions
> 4. Therefore, trait I is present in S at T.[17]
> (N).

This concept of indispensability is the major reason that the functionalist metatheory has acquired a reputation for conservatism; for if all social and cultural items are indispensable to the maintenance of an on-going system, there would appear to be no way in which social reform can be justified. This implication of the functionalist metatheory has in recent formulations been modified. Even if certain functions are indispensable to the maintenance of a society, any society, this does not mean that the structures or social institutions carrying them out are not interchangeable. The original motivation for Almond's functional model of the polity was to provide a device by which the very disparate political structures of western and developing nations could be meaningfully compared. The authoritative making of decisions, which occurs in all political systems, can be maintained by the disparate mechanisms of pronouncements by a tribal leader, decisions in cabinet, and the edicts of a governing Marxist party. The important thing to stress is the idea of the functional equivalence of a number of differing institutional structures.

The abandonment of many of the consequences of the organic analogy have led some, most notably Kingsley Davis, to conclude that functionalism is no longer a special method in sociology, but is identical with what might be called 'scientific sociology'. To Davis, the most commonly agreed upon definitions of functionalism make it synonymous with sociological analysis as such, and make non-functional synonymous with either reductionist theories or pure description.[18] In other words, sociology is about the relationship between parts of a society to the whole, and of one part to the other, and, not only is this what functionalism does, it is a definition of the scientific task in its quintessential form. The views of other methodologists of the social sciences serve to complement Davis' argument to some degree. Nagel, for instance, suggests, that once those uses of the term 'function' which fail on logical grounds are eliminated, what is left is the summation of a theory which is basically congruent with the methods of the natural sciences, that is to say with statements in which function means either a recognized utility or expected effect, or, alternatively, a statement about a more or less inclusive set of consequences that a given thing or activity has either for 'the system as a whole' to which the thing or activity supposedly belongs, or for various things belonging to the system.[19]

In one sense the argument of Davis and Nagel would appear to have some justification, but in another it is less cogent. What both are saying, in effect, is that the functionalist metatheory has generated a corpus of hypotheses which are, like those of the natural sciences, capable of evidential refutation. In other words, the functionalist model is capable of being transformed from mere insight into scientific theory in at least some instances. But despite this, functionalism in its metatheoretical orientation cannot be identified with sociological theory in general, since it persists in emphasizing its original, if somewhat modified, analogy as an heuristic tool of analysis. In this latter aspect, if functionalism is to be defended, it must be in respect of its ability to illuminate elements of social reality that are essential to any social and political analysis.

Functionalism and political insight

The ability of functionalism to offer insight into the world of political behaviour is a subject to which we have already devoted some attention. What were delineated as the elementary forms of the political life can also be regarded as the minimum functional imperatives in the absence of which no political existence would be conceivable. For political activity to occur there must be at least some degree of stability of expectations. Hobbes, after all, wrote not as a sociologist, but as political philosopher concerned with preventing anarchy within the state. A functionalist insight points to the elements of stability which must exist, but does not thereby preclude a study of politics which emphasizes the conflict of group or class interests. As we have noted more than once, class action is dependent on the existence of common group norms, and, indeed, the Marxists, whose devotion to a social theory of conflict is complete, are in fact the first to laud the virtues of 'class solidarity'. Moreover, any non-revolutionary conflict involves not a change in the normative pattern, but a desire on the part of some to usurp the existing role-players. Elections and coups d'état certainly involve conflict, but in a very real sense the order of the day is 'as you were'. Even the most dramatic, and outwardly successful, revolutionary redefinitions of normative patterns may be much less complete than they seem. It was Marx who noted that it was the haute bourgeoisie, who had hardly been a depressed class before the French revolution, and after it, constituted the effective ruling stratum in society, and it was Lenin, on his death bed, who had visions of an 'oriental restoration' of all that was most oppressive in Tsarist bureaucratic centralism. Functionalism does have the virtue of emphasizing these elements of stability, which can sometimes be ignored in the study of the white-hot passion expended by political role-players in advocating a little tinkering with the *status quo*.

The functionalist emphasis on stability is bound up in its insight that society has systemic properties. This concept of system is, of course, derived from the biological sciences, which picture the organism as a self-maintaining system, the maintenance of which is preserved by the performance of certain basic functions. Within this system are others like the endocrinal system and the nervous system, which through constant interaction and reaction with the organism's environment preserve a balance which is termed 'life'. The use of an organic system analogy in sociology or politics implies that society or polity are self-maintaining entities, and that they may best be understood by an analysis of their transactions with the environment and internal interactions directed to the end of self-maintenance. In strict terms, this analogy is immediately susceptible to criticism on the ground that, unlike the case of the biological organism, we possess no criterion of judgment for deciding whether societies or polities are *in extremis* because of a failure to perform given functions. Whatever else social and political systems do, they rarely die, as eventually must the biological organism. As most social systems change, and the apperception of such change in pseudo-survival terms must inevitably constitute a value judgment. On the other hand, we have noted that social and political arrangements change relatively slowly. The rigidities inherent in the ability of group identity to survive personal change, and the process of socialization to attach children to the outworn normative patterns of their elders, must be regarded as pointers to the existence of some systemic properties in the social world. At most such a system could be regarded as a moving equilibrium, but this does not give an *a priori* reason for the belief that an organic system analogy will be totally unilluminating.

One of the most important perspectives stemming from the analogy is that of the internal and external relatedness of social phenomena. Since an organic or quasi-organic system must carry out external transactions with its environment, the analogy suggests the importance of factors normally thought of as non-political in determining

the nature of the political life. The dependence of political phenomena on outside factors is by no means a novel perspective, and
different writers have suggested the primacy of economic, biological
and psychological determinants. Moreover, because the empirical
boundaries of political and social systems are well nigh impossible
to determine, the insight remains largely at an analytical level.
However, at this level, the system analogy stresses two important
features of transactions with the non-political. First, it does not imply
the primacy of any single external type of existential determination.
The organism, and by analogy the social and political systems, are
dependent on their total environment. To use the Parsonian framework of ideas, the political imperative of *goal achievement* is dependent not merely on the system's *adaptive* (economic) transactions
with the environment, but also on its ability to effect *tension management*, that is to control individual motivations insofar as they are
subject to stress, and *integration*, which relates to the system's
ability to cope with environmental stresses on valuative, normative
and technological orientations.[20] In other words, the systems
metatheory suggests a multi-causal, rather than mono-causal, search
for political explanation. Second, 'Cautiously applied, the concept of
system has the great virtue of forcing our attention to sets of interactions occurring within complex wholes that might otherwise be
overlooked. . .'[21] This point can be exemplified in the context of
Almond's developmental approach. The many types of input, output,
and conversion functions are all reciprocally interdependent. The
degree to which decision makers are capable of providing adequate
volumes of material outputs is dependent on the support that
individuals accord the existing structure of decision-making. As
Aron points out, there are problems inherent in a situation, like the
French, where strong demands for social welfare outputs are matched
by a strong tradition of minimal support in the form of massive tax
evasion.[22] From the point of view of determinate scientific explanations at the present time, this conceptualization of multitudinous
dependent variables makes for considerable empirical difficulties of
isolating causal relationships, but from the point of view of gaining
greater illumination of political complexity, it has much to offer.

The functionalist emphasis on the way in which structures and
institutions contribute to the maintenance of the system is manifestly
a result of its stress on the co-operative aspects of social reality. But
this idea of function, whatever part it plays in the different types of
system that have been advocated for political analysis, can be argued
to constitute a genuinely cumulative method for the study of political
phenomena in comparative contexts.[23] As Bernard Brown has
argued, the traditional approach to comparative politics does not

have this cumulative character.[24] To compare constitutions, legislatures, pressure groups and other structural entities is frequently to compare the incomparable. Legislatures, for instance, may do entirely different things; in the United States they may have a genuine decision-making role, in Britain their powers may have waned to a residual ability to 'advise, encourage and warn' and in the Soviet Union they may serve merely to legitimate the pronouncements of the Central Committee of the C.P.S.U. A comparison in functional terms, however, obviates this difficulty by comparing in terms of functions, which *ex hypothesi* are performed in all politics. This can be done by taking the various political functions and comparing the structural arrangements utilized for their performance, or by taking given structures and comparing the style of functional performance. An example of the latter is Roy Jones' comparison of the House of Commons and the United States Congress in terms of a modified version of Almond's conversion functions.[25]

	House of Commons	*Congress*
Demand articulation	Very low	Low
Demand aggregation	Low	Moderate
Rule making	Moderate	High
Rule application	Low	High
Rule adjudication	Very low	Low
Socialization	Moderate	Moderate
Recruitment	High	Moderate

It should be noted that, although these categories of comparison come from a systems model, there is no logical commitment to systemic analysis implied by their use in this way. All that is required is the acceptance that the delineated functions do in fact describe performances that most political organizations carry out. Indeed, it is another facet of metatheoretical formulations that they do not have to be accepted *in toto*. Insight does not require logical coherence to be useful, and we may accept some aspects of an analogy as being illuminating without being committed to others.

It is equally important to realize that a contention that a particular metatheoretical perspective is able to provide political insight does not imply that it will be equally illuminating in all political contexts. The argument that an organic system analogy may be useful in looking at societies and polities, which have a relatively coherent structure provided by normative patterning, does not mean that international politics, which for the most part lacks such patterning, can be usefully examined in terms of this conceptualization.[26] Nor does it mean that phenomena unamenable to insight from a particular metatheory will not be illuminated by others, as seemingly international politics is illuminated by the theory of games.[27]

Functionalism and change

The previous section has discussed some of the insights which stem from the functionalist metatheory's organic analogy and its concomitant emphasis on the co-operative basis of social and political life. There is, however, another side to the matter. Functionalism has been constantly criticized for its conservative orientation and consequent inability to illuminate processes of change, and, although some modern versions of the theory belie this criticism to a limited extent, it will become obvious that the criticisms are based on the truth that the theory does tend to concentrate overly on stability and co-operation.

As is so frequently the case in the social sciences, some of the criticism of functionalism stems from a confusion of the respective roles of the methodologies of faith and doubt. Critics demand of functionalist metatheory an evidential status it cannot provide, and these critics are encouraged by metatheoreticians who argue that their statements constitute scientific explanations. Such a confusion arises in the claim that functionalism is conservative in virtue of its use of teleological argument. Teleological arguments are those which attempt to explain a phenomenon in terms of its assumed purpose. Examples would be the assertion that heavy water exists in nature in order to provide man with the felicity of nuclear explosions, or that man has a nose on his face in order to provide the short-sighted with a projection on which to balance their spectacles. It is a teleological argument which forms the basis of the assumption of functional indispensability, which, as we pointed out, involves the logical fallacy of affirming the consequent. But to point out that teleology can lead to frightful howlers does not mean that its use cannot promote our understanding of otherwise incomprehensible phenomena. For instance, an analysis of Party congresses of the C.P.S.U. in functionalist terms might argue that they provide a means for the delegates to express and reinforce their sense of party solidarity. In other words, the significance of the phenomenon lies in its purpose. If the functionalist argued, as many might, that this constituted a scientific explanation of C.P.S.U. congresses, he would easily be proved wrong. The empirical regularity of congress attendance is explained by a number of factors including the desire of delegates for a free trip to Moscow, a desire for the prestige involved in delegate status and perhaps even some admixture of fear about the consequences of non-compliance with party directives. But the important point is not whether the functionalist argument constitutes a determinate explanation, but whether it illumines the nature of C.P.S.U. congresses. There can be little doubt that a focus on the functions of such gatherings tells us more about their nature than would an explanation in terms of the individual motivations for attendance. Furthermore, there need be no conservative presumption that the C.P.S.U. congresses are the only means of reinforcing party solidarity. A wide variety of different structural arrangements could realize this same end, but this is no reason why we should deny the insight of how such congresses do in fact operate.

This Russian example illustrates a further point in respect to the critique of functionalism as an apologia for the *status quo*. The undoubted emphasis on stability and mechanisms of social co-operation unquestionably lead to a concentration on processes which maintain the on-going system, but it does not point to the maintenance of any particular system, but rather to the maintenance of the system currently the subject of investigation. Thus the functionalist analysing the Soviet political reality is likely to focus on these mechanisms which preserve the current definition of 'socialist legality', as the American political scientist *cum* functionalist is likely to emphasize pluralistic mechanisms of conflict resolution. It is even possible by a 'mental experiment' to construct functional imperatives for any political system whose objectives are postulated. In reality, such a functional specification is the substance of the best utopian writing, and is exemplified by Plato's discussion of the education of the Guardians.

Obviously, where there is a built-in bias to processes which maintain on-going systems, the illumination of processes of change is likely to present difficulties. These problems can be exemplified by a brief examination of some of the frameworks which functionalism has advanced for the analysis of social change. One such framework is inherent in the interaction model of society advanced in Chapter 2. When one or more individuals are in an interactive situation they will develop a pattern of accepted behaviour regulated by normative expectations. This normative regulation may be seen as the simplest form of the Parsonian solution to the Hobbesian problem of order; the maintenance of social order is effected by delicate and complex mechanisms of social control. But behaviour which deviates from the accepted normative patterns can occur if the external situation of the interacting individuals alters in such a way that their expectations of one another are disturbed. For instance, the normative code regulating the relationship between teacher and pupil may be upset if the teacher attempts to impose middle class standards on the working-class child. Under these circumstances of role conflict, the working-class boy may reject middle-class standards and join a gang of others in a similar conflict situation. This gang will through interaction form a normative code by which the individual member may gauge his success and esteem in terms of the performance of gang exploits, rather than in terms of the scholastic attainment code of the middle-class milieu.[28] In other words, an analysis in terms of conflicting normative expectations is able to encompass the type of change implicit in the creation of delinquent or criminal sub-cultures within society.

What Parsons calls the 'structural differentiation approach' offers a further functionalist perspective on social change.[29] This approach delineates a model of components, or functions, of social action in terms of which individuals may feel strain if environmental circumstances alter. These components are *values*, which may be seen as the ultimate legitimations of social action; *norms*, which are more specific regulatory principles necessary to realize values; *mobilization for motivation*, which determine the forms of organization of human action, and *situational facilities*, which are the means of obstacles hindering or facilitating the achievement of goals. If one was to characterize the classical model of the democratic polity in these terms, it could be suggested that the value was democracy, the norms were free elections designed to realize that value, mobilization for motivation involved the organizational form of political parties which all were free to join, and the situational facilities were the material resources available to realize the voters' purposes. These components are ordered in terms of their conceptual level of generality; whereas an attack on democratic values necessarily undermines the other components, a conflict about the use of situational facilities need involve no other component but itself. Strain in such a system occurs when an alteration in the environment gives rise to deficits in the input of goal attainment for actors in the system. In time of war, for instance, individuals in a democratic system may temporarily abandon elections because such a normative device is irrelevant, and possibly dysfunctional, to their aim of victory. In other words, strain is removed by identifying the component of action in which it occurs, and restructuring the components until the strain is removed and a new balance achieved. The necessary condition of such a resolution of stress is the 'rational' identification of the sources of strain, and respecification of each component below it in order of generality. Where this does not occur, the solution is not likely to be of a type conducive to the removal of the strain.

Even if it be agreed that this metatheoretical model of change is useful, it may be necessary to introduce modifications in order to cater for social change which does not stem from a 'rational' respecification of the components of action. As Neil Smelser points out, the very fact of severe strain is conducive to a redefinition of social action in terms of a 'non-rational' generalized belief.[30] Such a belief has the function of redefining the actor's situation, but in a peculiar way which short-circuits the normal process of respecification of the components of action. Instead of looking for a solution at the next highest level of generality, it finds it ready-made at the highest level of generality, and instead of restructuring each component, it applies the ready-made solution immediately on the level at which the strain is manifest. In other words, the basic situation here is the postulation of an absolutely efficacious remedy to a perceived social problem. As an example of the type of social movement attempting to bring about change and motivated by a generalized belief, one might cite the nationalist movements which preach that with the coming of independence from the colonial aggressor all the problems of underdevelopment will magically disappear.[31]

All these functionalist schemes are useful insofar as they conceptualize the processes involved in the individual's perception of altering environmental situations, and stress that the desire for change may stem from individual desires to restore the securities of a previously existing situation, or an imagined 'golden age'. Even Marx could not resist the temptation of suggesting that Communism would, on a new and higher level, recreate the idyllic, unalienated life of primitive man. Nonetheless, each of these models betrays its origin in a cooperative metatheory. In all three, the focus of analysis is the existing system, and terminology like 'deviance' and 'non-rational respecification' indicate clearly that change is regarded as aberrant behaviour. As Jones notes of the political application of functional theory, the functionalist regards those changes which tend to be destructive of the existing political structure as basically non-political. A revolution or civil war may not necessarily be the subject of a negative value judgment, but insofar as it involves the destruction of the existing political community, it cannot be seen as a political event. The functionalist may be able to offer a coherent set of explanations as to why revolutions occur under specific circumstances, but, as Jones says, 'the actual process of revolution requires a fresh conceptual framework'.[32] Whether such a framework can be provided by a metatheory of conflict will be the subject of the next chapter.

The analysis of conflict as a metatheoretical orientation

It was the conclusion of our analysis of the functionalist metatheory that while its exponents could provide a number of approaches to the study of social and political change, their commitment to such an endeavour was less than complete. Since the basic orientation of the structural-functionalist is to those processes which maintain the social and political structure, there is a tendency to dismiss these processes that are destructive of the political system as being in some way non-political in nature. The usage of the term 'non-political', however, although it may accord well with the postulates of functionalist theory, is more than somewhat anomalous. In normal usage, change and conflict are regarded as being the stuff of politics. In the British political arena, the main event is the contest or conflict every five or so years between the two major political parties for office in the ensuing period. Between elections, what attracts the attention of the political analyst and political correspondent are the conflicts between groups of political role-players over varying policy issues. Similarly, in the field of international politics, the focus of interest is on the conflicts between nations, not on the rare instances when they reach agreement. Moreover, such a focus seems more than justified by the relative insignificance of the matters on which some degree of international accord has been reached. In contrast to the structural-functionalist school, the theorists we are now about to discuss emphasize conflict and change, rather than co-operation and stability. To many of these theorists of conflict a revolutionary upheaval of social and political structures is precisely what politics is about. To them not only are events like the Russian Revolution and the Vietnam War of a political nature, but they are exactly the sort of events that shape the political institutions of society. In other words, the conflict theorist denies the claim of the functionalist to understand the nature of society through its co-operative mechanisms, and suggests rather that we concentrate on social conflict, violence and coercion. Such theorists would tend to endorse the basic insight of Marx's statement that 'the history of all hitherto existing society is the history of class struggles', although for class struggles they might substitute power, religious or ideological conflicts.[1] Not all conflict theorists are united as to the causes of conflict and change, but all agree that these are the basic sociological processes.

The different perspectives of functionalist and conflict theorists have been formalized by Dahrendorf as two contrasting ideal types. In his view, we may look at the functionalist theory as resting on four fundamental assumptions:

(1) Every society is a relatively persistent, stable structure of elements.

(2) Every society is a well-integrated structure of elements.

(3) Every element in a society has a function, i.e., renders a contribution to its maintenance as a system.

(4) Every functioning social structure is based on a consensus of values among its members.[2]

In contrast, what we call the 'conflict approach', and what Dahrendorf calls the 'coercion theory of society', emphasizes a diametrically opposed set of assumptions:

(1) Every society is at every point subject to processes of change; social change is ubiquitous.

(2) Every society displays at every point dissensus and conflict; social conflict is ubiquitous.

(3) Every element in a society renders a contribution to its disintegration and change.

(4) Every society is based on the coercion of some of its members by others.[3]

Dahrendorf points out that the assumptions contained in both of these models are somewhat oversimplified and overstated, but insists that they encapsulate the basic differences between the two approaches to sociological analysis. Without contesting that this dichotomous set of assumptions may well describe the respective essences of functionalist and conflict theory, it is as well to remember that both models are ideal types of the utmost generality. In effect, they are 'one-sided accentuations' of metatheories, which, as we have stressed, are not without their element of bias in the first place. To discuss these contrasting models, however, does help to locate the respective roles of the two metatheories in illuminating social and political reality.

An important issue is raised by the manner in which Dahrendorf binds together each set of assumptions. In each case it would appear that he regards all four elements as essential to an integrated theory. Thus a functional theory must include stability, integration, functional co-ordination and consensus; a conflict theory must include change, conflict, disintegration and coercion. In reality, however, there would appear to be no logical connection between the first three assumptions of each model and the final one. The Parsonian analysis, starting as it does from the Hobbesian problem of order, does not necessarily take consensus of values as given, but rather may explain deviant behaviour in terms of a conflict over institutionalized norms. Nor necessarily does conflict theory presuppose coercion. Strangely enough, Dahrendorf's own theory of class conflict in industrial society is an illustration of this point. His argument, as we shall see, is that class conflict stems from the inevitable opposition of interests of those who wield authority and those who are subject to it. But authority in contradistinction to power is defined precisely by the fact that it is in some sense legitimate; that is, it is accepted by those over whom it is exercised.[4] Although this does not mean that those subjected to authority cannot have interests opposed to those in positions of domination, it would seem to mean that the relationship involved is not necessarily one of coercion, insofar as that term designates the use of external constraint to force the individual in a manner contrary to his desires. Moreover, in the case of the functionalist model, it would appear that the theorist need not be bound by the assumption of integration to the exclusion of that of conflict. Coser in analysing *The Functions of Social Conflict* is in fact pointing to the positive contributions made by conflict to the integration of social systems.[5] Finally, it should be noted that Dahrendorf's third assumption in his stability model, that 'every element in a society has a function', is a restatement of the postulate of universal functionalism long since abandoned by the more sophisticated adherents of the functionalist metatheory.

Dahrendorf makes one further observation about his models which, while on the surface it may appear paradoxical, in fact substantiates much of what has already been suggested about the nature of metatheoretical formulations. This paradox lies in the simultaneous assertion that the stability and conflict models are logically contradictory and yet both useful for the analysis of social facts. If these models constituted what we have called 'scientific explanations' this statement would be quite untenable. Two theories from which alternative predictions can be derived cannot both explain the relationship between a single set of empirical variables. On the other hand, two opposed metatheoretical formulations may provide illumination of differing aspects of a single empirical phenomenon. Indeed, Dahrendorf suggests that the models he outlines can be seen as complementary in one sense; a realistic understanding of social and political processes presupposes the use of both. As he says:

> It is evidently virtually impossible to think of society in terms of either model without positing its opposite number at the same time. There can be no conflict, unless this conflict occurs within a context of meaning, i.e., some kind of coherent 'system'. No conflict is possible between French housewives and Chilean chess players, because these groups are not united, or perhaps 'integrated into', a common frame of reference. Analogously, the notion of integration makes little sense unless it presupposes the existence of the different elements that are integrated.[6]

The complementarity of approaches here implied would appear to offer an accurate enough appraisal of the manner in which conflict and co-operative metatheories can mutually contribute to our understanding. One casts shadow where the other casts illumination and *vice versa*. Marxism points to the way in which changes in the economic structure promote social conflict and social change; functionalism illustrates the adaptive processes involved in providing an allocation of resources conducive to the maintenance of the ongoing system. But while it is true that the ideal analysis of society and politics would contain an admixture of both approaches mixed in a ratio related to the phenomenon under investigation, in practice this is extremely rare. We can point out that even Talcott Parsons, the arch-functionalist, commences his analysis by evidencing the substratum of conflict presupposed by human activity, but it must be noted that it rapidly ceases to play any major role in his theoretical edifice. The Hobbesian problem of order may be his starting point, his final resting place is the exclusive role of normative expectations in integrating society.[7] Similarly, Marx in analysing the conflict-ridden nature of capitalist society had necessarily to make some mention of the circumstances in which cohesive class groupings arose, but in virtually all his writings this topic is subordinated to an overwhelming interest in class conflict and its consequences. It is only in rare asides in polemical works that it is possible to gain some idea of his theory of class formation. His suggestion, in *The Eighteenth Brumaire*, that the French peasantry were unable to form a class conscious of its interests because of their 'merely local interconnection', is one example.[8] The similarity between this insight and the functionalist view that efficient political communication is a *sine qua non* of concerted political action is by no means accidental; it stems from a common focus on elements promoting social cohesion. This sort of similarity of analysis is not common, not because the use of one metatheoretical approach logically precludes the use of another, but because the focus of the theorist's attention tends to be dictated by his existential circumstances.[9] It is manifest that the Marxist emphasis on change and conflict was related to the tumultuous political and social upheavals heralded by the industrial and French revolutions. The idea of stability as the basic social form must have seemed somewhat distant to those who witnessed the massive growth of industrial enterprise, the decline of peasant ownership and the genesis of new forms of political participation. One way of making sense of the chaos of events was to see it, as did Marx, in terms of revolutionary conflicts making way for a more harmonious society. Another was to see contemporary social processes as an ordered progress in which social interaction was regulated through the free competition of the market. This latter model, which may be called 'utilitarian', was that espoused by the sociologist Spencer.[10] Yet another way of analysing contemporary events was to see the traumatic changes taking place as destructive of the social fabric.[11] What all these approaches have in common is an emphasis on change as the major problem area of social and political analysis, a perspective symptomatic of the realities of nineteenth-century life. In contrast, the western nations in the mid-twentieth century appear to have acquired a relatively high degree of stability. Revolutionary conflict seems to be a thing of the past, and even change in the incumbents of political roles appears to make little difference to the even tenor of political life. Under such circumstances, it is hardly surprising that the emphasis of social analysis in these western nations has for the most part shifted in such a way as to focus on the permanence and maintenance of existing structures. If this applies to the sociologists and political scientists that have examined American society in recent decades, it is equally true of these social anthropologists that were the originators of the functionalist school, for if primitive and modern societies resemble each other in one respect it is in regard to the stability of social structures. It is the societies intermediate between these two extremes that manifest change to a marked degree, and produce theorists of social conflict. This rather speculative generalization should be tempered by one major consideration. The last decade has seen something of a revival of the conflict perspective, and it is not impossible that this is a reflection of the emergence of new and important sources of dissensus in our society. The not infrequent suggestion that events like the French student revolt and the Czecho-slovak bid for a 'national road to socialism' are but symptoms of the instabilities created by the emergence of a monolithic and bureau-cratic state apparatus may provide pointers to the type of conflict situations that the social and political analysts of the future will find commonplace.

The substance of conflict and change

The concepts of conflict and change are by no means as simple as they appear, and an examination of the conflict metatheory requires some discussion of their more problematic aspects. Very early on we delineated 'perfect conflict' as a situation in which two individuals or groups are aware of each other's normative expectations, but because they have opposed ends are unwilling to take action to fulfil those expectations. In consequence it is possible to identify two essential criteria which must exist before a conflict situation can be said to exist: the opposition of ends and the abrogation of normative expec-tations. Such a definition would seem to differentiate what is usually called *competition* from conflict proper.

> Competition involves striving for scarce objects (a prize or a resource usually awarded by a third party) according to established rules which strictly limit what the competitors can do to each other in the course of striving; the chief objective is the scarce objective, not the injury or destruction of an opponent *per se*. A football game played normally according to the rules is competition *until* one or more players begin to assault one another in a manner forbidden by the rules; then it becomes a conflict.[12]

The relevant point here is the conception of struggle within the frame-work of established rules or normative expectations. Seemingly, this instance of struggle does not meet one of the criteria of perfect con-flict; there is no abrogation of normative expectations. This presents a considerable conceptual difficulty, since what virtually all modern conflict theorists choose to call 'institutionalized conflict' seems to be strikingly analogous to the competition situation. Institutionalized conflict occurs when two parties to a dispute set up or agree upon a set of rules through which their differences may in some sense be mediated. For instance, in contrast to the often violent conflicts between labour and management in the nineteenth century, today both sets of disputants belong to industrial organizations, trade unions and employers' organizations, that with the aid of govern-ment have instituted a whole series of mediating and arbitration mechanisms. Such mechanisms have implicit within them a set of rules or norms as to how disputes will be settled. Does this mean that we must call the struggles between labour and management in the twentieth century *competition* rather than *conflict*? This apparent absurdity can be resolved if we remember that normative expectations can relate to components of social action of varying levels of generality. In looking at the Parsonian framework of social action, it was noted that he posited four types of components of social action; namely values, norms, mobilization for motivation and situational facilities. Using the word norm in our sense to mean a set of expectations about the appropriate behaviour of a social actor in a given situation, it can be argued that such expectations exist in relation to each separate component. Taking the example, we have already given, of institutionalized conflict between labour and management, it might be analysed as follows:

1 Labour and management hold to common democratic values.

2 Labour and management have at the normative level instituted agreed procedures for the resolution of conflicts.

3 Labour and management disagree about the forms of organization that should exist. There is, in other words, a conflict over mobilization for motivation. A specific instance of such a dispute would occur where the labour side felt that it should have greater responsibility in personnel matters than it is at present accorded.

4 Labour and management are in conflict over the level of remuneration appropriate to each. There is a dispute about the division of resources, or situational facilities, awarded to each sector of industry.

As can be seen, at some levels of generality there are common normative expectations, while at others there is open struggle. Looked at from the perspective of a functionalist the value and normative components of social action appear to indicate stability, integration, functionality and consensus, whereas a concentration on mobilization for motivation and situational facilities indicates conflict, and by extrapolation from the situation, change, disintegration and coercion. An overview of the whole model indicates an admixture of conflict and stability, in other words, competition. Several points emerge from this discussion. Since, as we have seen, virtually every existential situation includes elements of both stability and conflict, a competitive model is possibly the most appropriate instrument for an analysis of empirical reality. There are, indeed, very few theorists as extreme as Marx, who postulated conflict in every one of the components of action. Not only did he argue that the working class was financially exploited by paying them less than the 'use value' of their labour (situational facilities), but also that the form of capitalist organization, factory production (mobilization for motivation), was the prime cause of that exploitation. Moreover, this exploitation was reflected in the normative order by the institution of free enterprise, which gave the capitalists the freedom to exploit and the workers the freedom to starve if they wanted to avoid exploitation, and in the value component by a democratic freedom which conceded all power to a 'ruling committee' of the bourgeoisie. In summary, it may be true, as Dahrendorf for one suggests, that 'group conflict is ubiquitous', but this general postulate is of less importance than a specification of the level at which conflict occurs. As will be later suggested, there are good reasons for believing that the consequences of conflicts about some components of action will be very different from the consequences of disputes about others.

The problems associated with the concept of change as it occurs in the conflict metatheory can be separated into two major issues.

1 The totality of structures   One problem is that of how we know a change has taken place. This may seem very straightforward. If a phenomenon X has a certain property Y, then change has occurred when Y is in some way modified. If for instance one is an addict to those sweets composed of many layers of coloured sugar, which the English call 'gobstoppers', one may note that its colour changes from red to blue. But this immediately suggests the anomaly, that in common parlance at least, a change in colour does not make a gobstopper any less a gobstopper. In other words, to change the phenomenon one must do more than change just one of its properties. To take a more appropriate example, Dahrendorf asks what would be a sufficient criterion to say that the Marxist model of capitalist society was no longer appropriate to describe the society in which we live. This model is composed of the following elements:

> (1) The commercial organization, (2) the co-operation of two groups of the population, (3) the fact that one of these groups simultaneously owns and controls the means of production, whereas (4) the other group has no property and is confined to 'merely' labouring, (5) their connection by the market, (6) the acquisitive principle, and (7) economic rationalism.[13]

If this definition is thought of as in some sense 'real' one of two conclusions must emerge. It is possible to argue, as did Marx, that a change in one of these properties is sufficient to invalidate the whole model. Marx's analysis of the rise of the joint-stock company, implying a separation of the ownership and control of property, leads him to the conclusion that this development, if continued, will involve the supersession of capitalist forms.[14] Alternatively, it could be argued, as did the majority of Marx's followers, that capitalism is only superseded when all its defining characteristics have disappeared. This latter view leads to the strange conclusion that any society organized on commercial lines is capitalist in nature. This whole paradox stems from the 'fallacy of misplaced concreteness', the mistake of regarding definitions as in some sense having a reality apart from the empirical phenomena they delineate.[15] As has already been suggested in another context, definitions only have a value insofar as they are 'useful instruments of description'.[16] A definition of a gobstopper that merely characterizes it by the property of redness is not useful, since it does not serve to differentiate it from other phenomena possessing the same property. As Dahrendorf notes, the Marxian definition of capitalism also lacks utility for the same reason. The elements of this definition may be divided into two distinct groups:

> On the one hand, we encounter factors that can be shown to
> be connected with industrial production, independent of its
> social, legal or economic context: for example, the
> participation in production of a controlling group and a
> subordinate group, economic rationalism, possibly some form
> of market economy . . . On the other hand, there appear in
> these definitions elements which characterize the particular
> form of industrial production displayed by the industrializing
> countries of Europe and North America in the nineteenth
> century: above all the union of ownership and control, but
> also the poverty of industrial workers and the profit motive.[17]

By a process of particularization and specification of the traditional definition of capitalism, one is able to arrive at an understanding of precisely the type of changes that have occurred in the intervening period. Both nineteenth and twentieth century societies are characterized by these features inherent in the nature of industrial production; both are industrial societies. However, where Marx's society was additionally characterized by a fusion of ownership and control of capital resources in a single hand, and by extreme poverty of the industrial workers, this is much less the case today.[18] Capitalist society has in this sense given way to another form. Whether that form be called 'industrial society' as such depends on whether in our time these features stemming from the nature of industrial production are overlaid by others which are not necessarily presupposed by that type of production. For instance, if we note the dominance of the bureaucratic form of organization in modern society, and at the same time maintain that there is no necessary connection between bureaucratic organization and industrialism, we might be justified in giving it the appellation of 'bureaucratic industrial society'.[19]

2 The totality of change A second problem of change is presented by those theorists of change, like Marx, who define change as revolutionary change. Because the only important change is the radical change which overturns the existing social and political structure at a single stroke, Marx in effect sees the structure of capitalist society as essentially static. Although he talks of a 'law of development' of capitalist society, this is little more than an unfolding process of the immanent tendencies of the factory mode of production. This is remarkably similar to the type of functionalist explanation which sees progress and change as a sort of moving equilibrium of the system analogous to growth processes in the organism. Moreover, a mode of analysis which makes its exclusive focus revolutionary change must necessarily fail to illuminate the less dramatic alterations that take place in society between revolutions. The moves away from the capitalist properties of the combination of ownership and control and the extreme poverty of the workers have been relatively gradual, but have, nonetheless, resulted in major structural changes. To take the latter issue only, it may be noted that the amelioration of working class conditions in Britain started with the Factory Acts of the mid-nineteenth century and proceeded through the stages of the Public Health Act of the seventies, the limited social service provisions of the Liberal government of 1906, right up to the implementation of the Beveridge Committee's report by the Labour government of 1945. None of these developments involved revolutionary violence, but resulted from enactments passed by the duly-elected House of Commons. Despite this 'inevitability of gradualism', there is an enormous gulf between the Chartist of mid-nineteenth century England and the 'I'm all right, Jack' automobile worker of today's industrial Midlands. Perhaps the greatest paradox presented by the metatheoretical models we are examining is that, for modern western nations at least, the functionalist is more realistic about change than the more extreme conflict theorists. Because the former accepts that the 'social organism' has processes analogous to growth he is sensitized to gradual processes of change, whereas the latter seems only aware of change when the mobs are out on the streets and violence is rampant. This is by no means to disparage the conflict approach. If one assumes that the functionalist metatheory gives more accurate insight into societies displaying relatively high degrees of stability, and the conflict metatheory provides comparable illumination of societies in turmoil, it would have to be agreed that the latter had the widest analytical scope in our day and age.[20]

The differential emphasis of the two metatheories on gradual and radical change is also manifested in their respective images of the ideal social form. Whereas the functionalist advocates pluralism, that is the unity in diversity provided by the conflict of different groups within the structure of a commonly accepted normative pattern of rules of the game, many of the conflict theorists advocate a communitarian society in which conflict has been wholly extirpated, and, presumably, change also. This is, of course, particularly true of the Marxian variants of conflict theory. As Dahrendorf points out, the heuristic purpose of the concept of class is to emphasize how conflict is generated by social structure. This was Marx's purpose in introducing the concept, and, in Dahrendorf's opinion, is the reason it should be retained; to both class implies conflict by virtue of the meaning of the word. Only one of Marx's later followers, Stalin, could have been guilty of originating the 'bastard' theory of 'non-antagonistic classes', but it should be noted that Stalin's conceptual error has its root in the Marxist metatheoretical perspective of change.

The causes of conflict and change

To Marx the causes of conflict and change were unequivocal.

> For almost forty years we have stressed the class struggle as the immediate driving power of history and in particular the class struggle between bourgeoisie and proletariat as the great lever of the modern social revolution.[21]

If the causes of change and conflict lie in the class struggle, that is itself caused and conditioned by the individual's relationship to the means of economic production.

> The essential condition for the existence, and for the sway of the bourgeois class, is the formation and augmentation of capital; the condition of capital is wage labour.[22]

A class to Marx is a group conscious of its economic interests and is defined by its role in the process of production. Conflict is generated between classes because of their necessarily differing economic interests. Those individuals who possess property necessarily exploit the class which does not. One class benefits from the existing relations of production, whereas the other would benefit from its overturn, and the consequent unfettering of new productive forces. Where this contradiction, or creative tension, becomes too great the exploited class rises and usurps the power in the state in order to release the new economic potential. It should be noted that Marx assumes a single line of conflict in society. The industrial conflict of owners and wage-labourers is carried into the political sphere in virtue of the fact that the ruling class utilizes the state as a mechanism for consolidating its domination.

> The executive of the modern State is but a committee for managing the common affairs of the whole bourgeoisie.[23]

This theory, whatever its value as a determinate explanation of all social and political conflict, has the major virtue of stressing the particular relationship of one element of social structure, the economic arrangements of society, and the types of conflict which arise in society. As we have mentioned in passing, this insight is the basis of one discipline within the social sciences, economic history, which demonstrates the extent to which economic variables effect historical change. Even if not all conflict is economically determined, there is considerable empirical evidence that much political behaviour is motivated by the struggle to acquire a greater share of scarce resources. It is difficult to believe, moreover, that the coincidence between economic and social changes in the eighteenth and nineteenth century, and the similar coincidence between efforts to secure economic modernization in the developing countries and endemic political instability, are merely accidental. However, an emphasis on the economic causes of conflict does not necessarily imply an analysis in terms of the individual's relationship to the means of production. An example of an economic conflict unrelated to class in this sense is provided by the institution of apartheid in South Africa.

> In spite of considerable effort by liberal socialist and Communist organizers, white wage-earners remain staunchly racialist, and always side with the employers against African wage-earners. Whatever we might think about the moral value of this attitude, a simple calculation shows that from the point of view of their own material interests, their behaviour is perfectly rational and cannot be described as prejudice. The whites constitute about one-fifth of the population, and consume about three-quarters of the national product. Should the available wealth be distributed in the way it is in Britain, let alone evenly, the great majority of the whites would be reduced to poverty because the product per head is low.[24]

In other words, the opposition of white and black in South Africa is not related to the division between property-ownership and wage labour, but to the existing distribution of wealth, and, contrary to the Marxist assumption, the two variables are not always connected.

The Marxist might save his position by suggesting that the white wage-earner's conduct is related to a 'false consciousness' fostered by the ruling capitalist class. However, the assumption of 'false consciousness' is introduced at the cost of making any predictions derived from the Marxist theory totally unfalsifiable, for if the predicted event takes place the theory is confirmed and if it does not it is not a consequence of the inadequacy of the theory, but of the unfortunate propensity of the masses to be misled.

In Marx's own view, such a 'false consciousness' was likely to be overcome by the force of economic circumstances, but in the works of his later disciples the supersession of the ideas of false prophets plays such a major role that it suggests causes of change completely divorced from economic factors. This is the implicit message of Lenin's argument that trade unions are not in themselves agents of a revolutionary consciousness, but of a spontaneity which demands an improvement, rather than a total reshaping, of existing social structures.

> We said that there could not yet be Social-Democratic consciousness among the workers. This consciousness could only be brought to them from without. The history of all countries shows that the working class, exclusively by its own efforts, is able to develop only trade union consciousness, i.e., it may itself realize the necessity for combining in unions, to fight against the employers and to strive to compel the government to pass the necessary labour legislation.[25]

The revolutionary consciousness necessary for the class struggle to take its pre-ordained form is to be provided by a dedicated band of professional revolutionaries. Such a view relegates economic determinism of conflict and change to the status of a necessary, but insufficient cause. The sufficient cause lies in the apperception of the world by a small group of revolutionary intellectuals, who possess the determination to change the world according to the image of their dreams.

A very similar point is made by Sorel when he suggests that the proletariat, by adopting a conscious policy of violence, can restore a situation of declining class conflict to its pristine purity, and so achieve Marx's postulated Communist utopia. He makes the following case:

> Marx supposed that the middle class had no need to be incited to employ force, but we are to-day faced with a new and unforeseen fact—a middle class which seeks to weaken its own strength. Must we believe that the Marxian conception is

> dead? By no means, for proletarian violence comes upon the
> scene just at the moment when the conception of social peace
> is being held up as a means of moderating disputes;
> proletarian violence confines employers to their role of
> producers, and tends to restore the separation of the classes,
> just when they seemed on the point of intermingling in the
> democratic marsh.[26]

What is being said here is that the utilization of violence can itself be a cause of conflict, and that therefore individuals have it within their power to promote conflict by a conscious effort of will. Some of the contemporary doctrines of the revolutionary student movement share something of Sorel's ethos of violence. It is suggested that if students require evidence of the repressive society in which they find themselves, they should merely attempt violent provocation on the streets and so provoke the guardians of the law. Very rapidly, it is argued, the thin veneer of civilized impartiality will disappear, and the police will act as the heavy-handed guardians of ruling class privilege they really are. It should be noted that this argument is framed in such a way as to be totally incapable of empirical falsification. Since we may reasonably assume that the guardians of law and order are likely to react violently to such provocations as being showered with paving-stones, it is quite impossible to impute to them the role of lackeys of the ruling class, rather than mere annoyance with the student's immediate conduct. In other words, this modern dogma of student activism is in the nature of a 'self-fulfilling prophecy'. The fact that the argument is unamenable to falsification does not, of course, make it necessarily untrue, but the students might be advised to adopt the Ghandian strategy of non-violent protest, if they wish to convince a sceptical older generation.

It is becoming apparent that the causes of conflict and change are many and varied in kind. The relationship to the means of production, differential distributions of wealth, ideological perceptions and the conscious use of violence can all play a causative role. In theory, at least, this list could be extended indefinitely. It would seem that the causes of disagreement and conflict are as many as the types of social relationships the individual can enter. This is logically presupposed by the reciprocity of social interaction on which our whole analysis is based. Any interaction leads to a set of normative expectations, and while it is possible for a group of individuals to observe this normative pattern, it is equally possible for one or a number of them to diverge from the strict observance of those expectations; for every area of agreement there is a corresponding cause for disagreement. However, we will discuss one further theory as to the causes of conflict; namely,

Dahrendorf's theory that class conflict is a ubiquitous phenomenon in all imperatively co-ordinated associations. Such associations are those which are regulated by means of authority relationships. In modern society the range of such associations is very wide, including the State itself, industrial organizations, religious communities of faith and trade unions. Within each of these associations are status-roles conferring authoritative domination and subjection; some have the obligation to make decisions and others the obligation to obey them. In this dichotomy lies an objective conflict of interests, which may or may not be manifested in actual struggle. By utilizing a conflict model which is based on the possession or exclusion from authority, Dahrendorf axiomatically postulates the existence of only two classes in any specific conflict. His is a 'zero-sum' conception of authority; the possession of authority on the part of one status-role automatically presupposes the exclusion from authority of another status-role.[27] This whole argument of Dahrendorf's is just as much metatheoretical in nature as the functionalist suggestion that most human activities function to promote the on-going system. The basic proposition of his conflict model is quite untestable.

> Of the two aggregates of authority positions to be distinguished in every association, one—that of domination—is characterized by an interest in the maintenance of a social structure that for them conveys authority, whereas the other— that of subjection—involves an interest in changing a social position that deprives its incumbents of authority.[28]

This view is impossible to refute, since Dahrendorf states (1) that such interests may remain latent, and (2) the only empirical evidence that could be adduced for the existence of this postulated conflict of interests would be their manifestation in actual conflict. Dahrendorf explicitly recognizes the unscientific status of his assumptions, and justifies them in terms of the insight they provide.

> If we are concentrating in this study on the 'negative' functions of authority, we do so because this aspect is more appropriate and useful for the analysis of structurally generated systematic social conflict.[29]

Conditions of conflict and change

It should be emphasized that Dahrendorf maintains that class conflict generated by the authority structure of imperatively co-ordinated associations is by no means the only variety of conflict. International conflict cannot be seen in these terms for precisely the same reason that it is unamenable to analysis in terms of an organic systems model, that is, because of the non-existence of normative patterns in terms of which there could be an authoritative allocation of values. Dahrendorf in company with most other modern social scientists, and in contradistinction to Marx, sees social and political reality as being explicable only in multi-causal terms. Nor does the modern sociologist argue, as did Marx, that the conditions and form of conflict are in any way determinate. To the historical materialist, an understanding of individual's relationships to the means of production determined every aspect of the conflict situation including its result. The capitalist mode of production implied the formation of antagonistic classes based on capital and wage labour, and this antagonism implied the eventual supersession of the former class by the latter in a revolutionary upheaval leading to the 'truly human society' of Communism. According to this view, there is only one form of significant social conflict and only one condition for its appearance, the accumulation of wealth in the hands of private persons. Marx admitted that this model was ideal typical in kind, when he said:

> In a general investigation of this kind it is always assumed that real conditions correspond to their conception, or, which is the same thing, the real conditions are presented only insofar as they express their own general type.[30]

This does not, however, alter the fact that he conceived of the total process of social conflict and change as one determined by economic forces.

In contrast to this view, Dahrendorf and others maintain that the nature and effects of social conflict are dependent on the empirical situation in which it occurs. This can be illustrated by Dahlke's analysis of race riots. In a study of this subject he outlines a set of highly specific empirical conditions which in conjunction make the likelihood of such disturbances extreme:

> (1) That the period concerned is one in which change and mobility are dominant.
> (2) The minority has some trait or characteristic which can become the basis of negative assessments. E.g., skin colour, place of worship, etc.
> (3) The government or other lawful authorities assign the minority group an inferior status. E.g., the Jews in Nazi Germany, the Japanese in America (1941–5), the Indians in East Africa today.

(4) One or more major associations or organizations direct the attack against the minority.
(5) The press and other media have been minority-baiting.
(6) Suitable personnel (students and marginal workers) are available for initiating action.[31]

Dahlke's theory has been cited in detail because it provides a good example of the way in which a general conflict orientation can be translated into a series of hypotheses which are empirically falsifiable. Whether these six conditions constitute a necessary and sufficient explanation for the occurrence of race riots can be determined by examining instances when all occur, and comparing them with instances in which only some are present. However, even when the specification of empirical conditions is as precise as this, some problems remain. The determination of the attitude of the lawful authorities, for instance, is not a simple objective issue. The determination of an inferior status is dependent on the subjective appraisals of those concerned. To take the instance of the coloured minority in Britain, there can be no question that the government has no overt intention of assigning minority groups an inferior status, nor that it believes it has done so by a policy of restricted immigration. Moreover, those white groups that oppose coloured immigration could not possibly imagine that the authorities supported them, simply in virtue of the fact that these groups do not think that the government is doing sufficient to prevent it. On the other hand, it is more than probable that large groups of migrants themselves feel they are being assigned an inferior status. Since they are almost bound to attribute the prejudice they meet to the government's lack of energy in combating it, and since their dependents are subjected to numerous official restrictions before they are allowed to enter the country, it is very difficult for them to think of themselves as anything other than second-class citizens. It is perfectly within the reach of social science methodology to determine subjective attitudes, but the point that is being emphasized is that it is necessary to be aware that the intentions of one party to an interaction may be misinterpreted by another before such a methodology can be employed.

The type of variables that Dahlke discusses are highly specific to a given situation, but there are more general conditions that appear to influence the form of conflict and its outcome in a wide range of cases. These conditions can be usefully examined by looking at them in relation to the major dimensions of conflict activity outlined by Dahrendorf. Among the dimensions of conflict activity he suggests are important are the formation of conflict groups, the intensity of conflict, which is determined by the cost of defeat to the contending parties, the violence of conflict, that is the weapons the combatants choose, and the effect of conflict on social structure. In each case, it will be the empirical conditions which determine where along these dimensions a conflict situation will lie.

Among the most important conditions is the degree of communication and information that the contending parties experience. Indeed, whether they contend at all is a function of whether they possess sufficient information to realize the opposition of their interests to those of other parties. As we have already noted, Marx explained the French peasants' inability to comprehend his situation in class terms as a concomitant of the 'merely local interconnection' between them. Geographical dispersion and isolation can, in other words, prevent individuals coming together to articulate their common interests. Modern techniques of communication have for the most part obviated this difficulty, but it might be suggested that it has remained one of the major factors so far preventing the appearance of a militant independence movement in Papua and New Guinea, which would present enormous topographical and linguistic difficulties. Equally, the well-known difficulty of forming consumer pressure groups may be surmised to arise from the fact that consumer-status presupposes no significant set of social interactions or communication between those of similar interests. Moreover, the degree of information possessed by contending parties once formed may be crucial in determining both the intensity and violence of conflict. A lack of information about the intentions of one's opponent and others peripherally involved in the conflict situation may lead to an unrealistic appraisal of the type of weapons that should be used. This is illustrated by the mistaken assumption of both France and Britain in 1956 that the values of the United States in regard to the Middle East were not incompatible with their own. This led them to use weapons of conflict in the Suez situation that would have been unthinkable had they realized the degree of American antagonism to any policy of direct intervention. Had Britain and France had adequate information, they would almost certainly have attempted some form of mediation with Nasser, rather than choose the ill-fated course of 'armed conflict'.[32] It should not be thought in this context that the intensity and violence of conflict are always positively correlated. An awareness of information regarding the high cost of defeat may deter the combatant from adopting violent weapons of conflict. Thus the small businessman does not indulge in massive price-cutting, because he is well aware that the cost of defeat is bankruptcy. Obviously, however, the opposite situation also occurs, and the high cost of defeat makes both sides increase the degree of violence. This situation is known to the Cold War strategists as 'escalation'. Since the degree of information available to the conflicting parties about the cost of defeat can either increase or decrease the violence exhibited, no *a priori* assumptions can be made about unknown circumstances, and for an understanding of the consequences of an improved information-flow empirical investigation would be required.

The conditions under which political organization is possible in a given society are also a major determinant of the dimensions of conflict. This factor is extremely important in regard to the possibility of group formation and the degree of violence exhibited. All political communities exercise some control of the group life within them. During the second world war, British fascist groups were disbanded and the Communist Party was for a time banned. The Public Order Act of 1936, which was enacted to combat the influence of the former, prevents the formation of para-military groups and the wearing of uniforms by private bodies. Naturally, the totalitarian polities are the worst offenders in this respect, and, indeed, it may be suggested, that the suppression of independent groupings constitutes one of the defining characteristics of such systems.[33] Under these circumstances, manifest conflict is a very rare occurrence. However, where it does occur, it tends to be very violent in character. The Hungarian revolution and the guerrilla warfare conducted by partisan groups in the second world war provide sufficient illustration of this point. Where the cost of defeat involved in the actual formation of a group is equal to the cost of utilizing the most violent weapons of conflict, a society retains no deterrent power once the initial step of group formation is taken. The suppression of manifest conflict should not be confused with the suppression of social change. Since the authorities are usually perfectly well aware of the dangers of violence stemming from the suppression of interest groups, they may take steps to appease interests prior to their dramatic statement in violent form. This would, for instance, appear to have been the motivation for Stalin's letter 'Dizziness from Successes', which called a halt to the worst excesses of the collectivization programme of the late 1920s.[34]

The degree to which lines of social conflict coincide in a given society is a further important condition shaping conflict situations. In Dahrendorf's model of class conflict in an industrial society, there is no assumption that lines of conflict will extend beyond the bounds of a single imperatively co-ordinated association. There may be conflict within industry and not within the State. There may be disputes between incumbents of authority positions and those subject to them in trade unions and religious organizations, but neither in logic presupposes a more general state of conflict within society. Where conflict is restricted to a single institutional sphere the cost of defeat to the participants is relatively low, since they are involved in it only in respect of one of their many status-roles. In the institutional setting of the industrial firm, the employer and shop steward may be implacably opposed, but should both be officials of the local sports club there is no necessary reason why their animosity should be carried over to the new context. It should be noted that all socio-logical theories of conflict posit this structural determination of animosity, rather than a psychologically induced aggressiveness to persons. When Bakunin said that freedom would only be achieved by man 'when the last king was strangled with the guts of the last priest', he did not thereby imply that kings or priests were necessarily unpleasant persons, but that their structural role was an impediment to the achievement of a desirable form of social organization.

Where conflicts within one social organization are unrelated to those in others, the situation may be described as one of *pluralism*. An opposite situation occurs when the incumbents of authority positions in one association occupy similar positions in other organ-izations. This was the situation Marx described, when he suggested that the owners of industry were in another guise that of the bour-geoisie, the masters of the state and indeed the controllers of the ruling ideas of the epoch:

> The ideas of the ruling class are in every epoch the ruling ideas, i.e. the class which is the ruling material force of society, is at the same time the ruling intellectual force. The class which has the means of material production at its disposal, has control at the same time over the means of mental production, so that thereby, generally speaking, the ideas of those who lack the means of mental production are subject to it.[35]

In Marx's day, there was a distinct superimposition of lines of con-flict. In the industrial sphere, the entrepreneur had absolute control of the economic fate of the wage-workers; in the State, it was the pro-pertied and monied that made decisions, and even within the religious community there was some tendency for the propertied to belong to the Established Church, while the workers were non-conformists in persuasion. Under these circumstances, conflict situations involve an extremely high cost of defeat, since the individual is implicated in respect of virtually every one of his manifold status-roles. As Coser notes, 'the total personality involvement of group members makes for mobilization of all sentiments in the conduct of the struggle'.[36]

These concepts of pluralism and the superimposition of lines of conflict need not be restricted to class conflicts, but may be applied to the totality of conflicts within a given social structure. It may be argued that the likelihood of political conflict is increased whenever lines of struggle fail to overlap. Thus Belgian political crises are related to the fact that the French-speaking sector of the population tends to be Catholic in faith and urban in location, while the Flemish speaking group tend to be Protestant in belief and rural in location. This is a situation in which interaction exists in virtue of common nationality, but in respect of little else. It is worthy of note, that the factor which differentiates Northern Ireland from the rest of the United Kingdom is a superimposition of religious and political beliefs.

The degree of social mobility that exists within the social structure is a further determining condition of the intensity of conflict. Where classes are 'closed' the only manner in which individuals can change their position is by a change in the nature of the authority relations themselves. However, where classes are more 'open' to aspirants for a higher status, there will be a tendency to compete with others to achieve a superordinate position. In this sense, a high degree of social mobility is destructive of conflict group solidarity, and the cost of defeat is diminished for the individual to the extent that he does not see his life chances as exclusively determined by his membership of a particular group. As so often before, the most important issue here is that of the perception, rather than the reality, of mobility. The rates of social mobility in Britain and the United States are rather similar, but the extent to which conflict groups have been formed to alter structures of authority is markedly different. In contrast to the majority of European nations, in which working class parties have played a predominant role in twentieth century political activity, the United States has failed to produce a labour party on any significant scale. This paradox appears to stem from a differential perception of the degree of social mobility possible. Just as, according to Napoleon, every Frenchman has a field-marshal's baton in his pocket, so according to American popular belief there is always the chance of rising 'from rags to riches', and while that chance persists for the determined and intelligent man (and who isn't in his self-perception?), it seems pointless to bring down the authority structure which confers the riches. Quite apart from these considerations, there is a tendency in modern industrialized societies for the degree of social mobility to increase. Since in such societies many of the authority positions in bureaucratic organizations are awarded on the meritocratic criterion of educational aptitude, and since education is increasingly open to individuals of all social strata, it must be assumed that inter-generational mobility at least is increasing, and with it the intensity of conflict will diminish. This diminution in the intensity of conflict stemming from educational mobility is not necessarily an unmixed virtue, since high mobility does not imply the disappearance of conflict groups, whereas meritocratic mobility does imply the creaming-off of talent from those groups promoting the interests of those in subordinate positions.[37]

The existence of mechanisms for the resolution of conflicts once they arise can be an important variable in deciding the severity of struggle. As Dubin argues, continuous conflict between groups implies some degree of institutionalization.[38] Although conflict presupposes a dispute over normative arrangements, its continuance itself constitutes a relationship or interaction between two or more parties, which leads to new normative patterns emerging to regulate the sphere of conflict. This may even extend to some abstract agreement between the parties as to the shared values by which they evaluate conflicting ends. Dubin notes a number of examples of such values in the sphere of industrial relations:

> An individual worker should not be subjected to arbitrary action by the supervisor . . . Wages should bear some logical relationship to an objective standard like locality or industry levels or movements in the cost of living.[39]

Apart from values, more concrete arrangements may be entered into by the contending parties. Examples would be the Nuclear Test Ban Treaty, or the arrangement entered into by Cuba and the United States for the return of hijacked aircraft. Moreover, repeated conflict often leads to regularized procedures for its resolution. Regular and predictable moves are made by both parties. The trade union makes its demands and negotiations between the two sides of industry ensue. If they meet with no success some form of arbitration or mediation by an outside party may be invited, and only when this in turn fails are the most violent weapons of all brought out, the strike and the lock-out. This institutionalized progression in the use of increasingly more violent weapons of conflict is an instance of the manner in which regularized interaction between conflict groups may turn physical manifestations of conflict into a last resort. In most modern societies there are, in fact, institutions, whose primary function is the resolution of conflicting issues. The decision-making apparatus of government is looked at in this light by the functionalist theorists of politics. The conversion functions may be seen as a device by which the conflicting demands of social groups are transformed into policy proposals which can be decided on by the representatives of the entire community.

A final condition is involved in the relationship between the dimensions of social conflict and the type of resultant social change. Dahrendorf suggests that this relationship can be expressed in the form of two equations:

1 The higher the intensity of conflict (cost of defeat) the greater will be the radicalness of structural change.

2 The more the violence of conflict (weapons chosen) the greater will be suddenness of structural change.[40]

The basic argument of the first equation is that the greater the involvement of individuals in a conflict, the more far-reaching their demands are likely to be, and consequently the more radical will be the results stemming from the conflict. This is illustrated by the Russian revolution in which the total involvement of the revolutionists was translated into a complete overturn of the social and political structure. In contrast, where individuals are only involved in conflict about a single institutional sector, that is where the cost of defeat is relatively low, their demands are more likely to be restricted in scope. In explaining the connection between the violence of conflict and the suddenness of change, Dahrendorf postulates the existence of three modes of change. These are defined by the degree to which change involves the replacement of governing personnel. The most sudden type of change is that which occurs when the total governing personnel is replaced. This is again exemplified by the Russian Revolution, where only the use of extreme violence made such a change possible. More commonly change occurs when only some of the ruling personnel are displaced. This is what occurs in elections in western democratic nations. The elected representatives come and go, but those filling executive and judicial posts go on for ever. Least sudden are changes that occur without any change in the ruling personnel. These occur when the ruling group as a result of conflict incorporates the proposals and interests of the opposition into its own policy. This is the type of change most commonly arrived at by institutionalized forms of conflict. The agreement by the Prices and Incomes Board that an increase in wage-levels is justified does mean that the ruling group incorporates the workers' demands into their policy, but it does not involve any change in the incumbents of political status-roles. Indeed the institutionalization could be seen as a means of effecting change without causing redundancies. It can also be used as an illustration that the suddenness and radicalness of structure change vary independently of each other. The institution of mechanisms of conflict resolution in western nations in the last century must itself be regarded as an extremely radical structural change, but it is one which has proceeded very gradually and with only slight changes in the governing personnel. This independence of suddenness and radicalness of change may offer some sort of solution to the recurrent difficulty experienced by social scientists in attempting to define what constitutes a revolution. In normal speech, we think of a revolution as a political upheaval of great suddenness and accompanied by extreme violence. This was certainly the case in both the French and Russian revolutions. But social scientists have talked of the industrial and managerial revolutions, both of which events took decades, if not centuries, to complete. But what these revolutions and the French and Russian ones have in common is their extreme radicalness of structural change. It would appear from this argument that, contrary to popular belief, revolutions are defined by their intensity of conflict and radicalness of change, rather than by their violence and suddenness.

Conclusion

In this chapter, in contrast to the last, no explicit attempt has been made to illustrate that the insight of the conflict theorist is valuable to political studies. This is because such a proposition is as evident to the political scientist as is the proposition that we must understand the processes by which expectations become institutionalized in order to understand social action to the sociologist. What has been emphasized is that the outlook which stresses the ubiquitousness of conflict in all social phenomena is as much metatheoretical in nature as the functionalist perspective. Oddly enough, however, the contradictory metatheoretical approaches we have looked at do not generate incompatible descriptions of social and political reality. This may be illustrated by comparing the views on value conflict espoused by Coser and Marx. The former suggests that conflicts over basic values are likely to be dysfunctional in respect of system maintenance, whereas conflicts over other components of social action are likely to promote useful adaptations of structure. That a functionalist should come to this conclusion is hardly surprising, since the overarching values of a society are the criterion which defines its continued existence. In a sense, the argument of the extreme conflict theorist like Marx is exactly contrary to this view. Since the worth of any change in the components of social action is related to a social structure (communism) which has yet to come into existence, the alteration of basic values is the *sine qua non* of a favourable evaluation of change. Equally, since the Marxist tends to regard minor changes as a means by which the ruling class strengthens its strangle-hold, they are hardly thought of as changes at all. This contrast may be represented as follows:

	Value change	*Non-value change*
Functionalist	Dysfunctional	Functional
Marxist	Progressive	Reactionary

If, however, this contrast is stripped of its evaluative emphasis, its metatheoretical perspective, a basic similarity emerges. Both the Marxist and the functionalist would endorse the description of value change as destructive of existing social structures, and both would argue that minor changes improve the system's capacity to survive.

	Value change	*Non-value change*
Functional	Destructive of existing	Conducive to system
Marxist	social structure	maintenance

This contrast and convergence makes a suitable conclusion to our examination of these metatheoretical approaches of co-operation and conflict. It should be readily apparent that these approaches shed illumination on different aspects of the same social phenomena. The fact that in substantive terms they come to remarkably similar conclusions should be a cause for optimism about the eventual emergence of a social science which is willing to include the insights of both metatheoretical perspectives.

Anomie and the theory of mass society

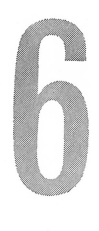

The substantive similarity of co-operative and conflict metatheories in regard to the likely effects of varying types of social change is not the only point at which the perspectives show a convergence of emphasis. Both approaches also share basically optimistic views about the nature of social progress. This distinguishes them quite radically from those who in a sociological context emphasize the prevalence of anomie, and in the political context stress the emergence of mass forms of political activity. The contrast of optimism and pessimism derives from a human evaluation of the social worth of the processes which the social scientist sees as most relevant to the analysis of contemporary society. The functionalist and conflict theorist in discussing respectively processes of stability and change are dealing with social mechanisms to which they attribute a very positive value. An analysis which demonstrates the importance of co-operative mechanisms cannot fail to bring forth optimism of he who approves of the basic structure of existing society. Equally, an emphasis which points to the ubiquity of forces promoting conflict and change cannot but please the analyst who looks forward to the coming of the 'truly human' society. But the theory of anomie and mass society points neither to social stability nor to social change of any positive kind, rather it emphasizes the existence of a process of social disintegration. Since the idea of disintegration in contradistinction to that of change implies no vision of a new and reconstructed reality, but only of the loss of a formerly existing state of social coherence, it is both nihilistic and profoundly pessimistic. One cannot say of social disintegration what Bakunin, the anarchist, said of social conflict and change: 'The destructive urge is in reality a creative urge.'

This difference between approaches based on conflict and anomie can be inferred from the definitions we offered of these phenomena. Perfect conflict occurs when two or more individuals or groups have a perfect awareness of each other's social expectations, but are equally unwilling to fulfil them. The most obvious reason for such an occurrence arises from the incompatibility of individual or group ends. But the very fact that the participants in such a conflict situation have ends or normative patterns they value has a number of implications. The first is that such norms can themselves form the basis for new types of social interaction. The disputing individuals or groups can band together with those of like disposition and outlook to promote the ends they desire. The second implication lies in the fact that a given conflict need not be disruptive of an on-going relationship. The areas of the individuals' agreement may be greater than those of their disagreement, and in consequence they may be in the happy position of being able to agree to disagree. Moreover, they may, as we have already seen, be able to institutionalize their dispute over limited ends by setting up some commonly-accepted mechanism of conflict resolution. In other words, social conflict is not destructive of social interaction *per se*, and one might even go so far as Simmel and argue that: 'While antagonism by itself does not produce sociation, it is a sociological element almost never absent in it.'[1] Perfect anomie, however, was defined as a situation in which, rather than accepting or rejecting the expectations made of him, the social actor is incapable of understanding what is expected of him. Instead of there being as in the case of social cohesion a common end of social action, or in the case of social conflict a divergence of ends, there is in the case of anomie no end at all. A situation of anomie is, in other words, one in which there is an absence of normative patterning; it is by definition a situation in which social interaction does not exist. In relation to a total society, it refers to a 'condition in which many persons in a social system have a weakened respect for some social norm or norms'.[2] The phenomenon of anomie causes pessimism to sociologists whatever their metatheoretical complexion, since it is in essence a negation of the subject-matter of their studies. It is not merely a question of anomie being destructive of existing social relationships, but of it being the antithesis of all social interaction. The individual who has no normative conceptions whatsoever cannot be a meaningful participant in the society in which he lives, nor can he be the creator of a new society.

This contrast of the pessimism of an approach which imputes the existence of a high degree of anomic behaviour, and those approaches which more optimistically stress stability and conflict, is not the only difference which sets apart an analytical theory that emphasizes the relative normlessness of social behaviour. Such a theory is necessarily more specific in its range of application than either functionalist or conflict theory. That this is the case stems from the logical impossibility of conceptualizing an on-going social system totally imbued by anomic patterns of behaviour. No such impossibility exists in visualizing a completely stable society in which all activities are functionally integrated, although, of course, no such society has every seen the light of day. Moreover, the assumption of perfect conflict only requires that we think of two highly antagonistic groupings sharing a common geographical location. The fratricidal struggle of civil war indicates that while parallels to the situation of perfect conflict may be rare, they are by no means inconceivable even at an empirical level. The point that is being emphasized is that while it is possible for the functionalist theorist to stress only elements of social stability, and the conflict theorist to stress only elements of instability, it is quite impossible for the theorist of anomie to stress only normlessness. To interpret the history of all hitherto existing society in terms of the ubiquity of anomie would be to make the nonsensical assertion that society had never existed. In consequence, the theorists who stress normlessness only do so in a limited context. They specify the particular circumstances under which their analytical tool provides an appropriate insight into social reality. Four such circumstances may be remarked:

1 In particular historical epochs. Here a specification is made by contrasting periods of social disintegration with periods of relative social cohesion.

2 In particular parts of society. Here the contrast lies in the adherence to normative patterns by some social groupings and the relative normlessness of other groupings. It is in this contrast that we find the distinction between the political elite and the masses that constitutes the basic rationale of the theory of mass society.

3 In particular situations. A specification is made in this case by contrasting situations in which individuals behave in a manner regulated by social norms and others in which this does not occur. The behaviour of individuals in crowds is frequently instanced as an example of this variety of anomic behaviour.

4 In particular types of society. A contrast is often made between the degree of normlessness of one type of existing society and the normative integration of another. This type of contrast has found its way into comparative politics as a fundamental insight on what distinguishes stable and unstable politics.

Since, as we have argued, it is impossible to be exclusively a theorist of normlessness and social disintegration, what we find is that the theorists of both stability and conflict utilize the concept of anomie, and more particularly of the normless mass, to offer explanations of features of social reality that cannot be easily fitted into their respective metatheories. Bramson makes this point very clear in identifying the central idea of both models in the concept of order, and in suggesting that to analyse disintegration both have utilized a new and common approach.

> Although the concept of order is central, there are those who wish to preserve a given social order, and others who wish to change it. But the politics of sociology of conservation and the sociology of change will always be the politics of order, not of anarchy. The preoccupation with social disintegration is continuous up to the present day, and culminates in the European theory of mass society.[3]

Some preliminary observations may be made about this common emphasis on normlessness as an explanation of social disintegration before looking at some of the more substantive theories constituting this approach. Although no social situation can be thought of as totally anomic, this does not mean that a perspective based on this concept cannot illuminate social and political activity. Just as it is possible to imagine individuals agreeing or disagreeing over the ends of social action, it is conceivable that there will be a lack of comprehension of others' ends, or indeed, in some situations, a complete lack of normatively defined ends. At least on the surface, the aimless violence sometimes exhibited in crowd situations appears to fit such a description very well. It is arguable that the lack of a common normative pattern in such a social aggregate is conducive to the acceptance of the first idea which comes along, irrespective of the degree to which it conflicts with normal and 'civilized' codes of social conduct. To look at the abrogation of traditional codes of conduct involved in the rise of totalitarian political movements in these terms seems to offer at least a hope of furthering political understanding.

But despite this promise of political insight, we must be prepared to find that some of the phenomena described as instances of anomie and mass activity are very different in nature. Since both theorists of stability and conflict tend to have an exclusive attachment to the one kind of interpretation of social reality, they often see evidence of the non-fulfilment of their theories as instances of social disintegration, rather than as proof that their metatheoretical formulations are in some sense one-sided. The Marxist, for instance, prefers to see the proletariat disintegrate into a normless, or 'falsely conscious', mass-man manipulated by the capitalist controlled mass media, rather than admit that at least some elements of the working class have been integrated into the existing framework of industrial society. As John Rex points out, the functionalists are guilty of an exactly analogous error in attributing anomie to what may well be the result of social conflict. As he says:

> One finds that the doctrine that 'strikes are due to misunderstanding' has great prevalance in modern industrial sociology. We should say that it would be more profitable at least to examine whether strikes could not be understood as a case of social conflict.[4]

One of the most important tasks in examining the metatheoretical approach of the theorists of anomie and the mass society will be the delineation of those circumstances in which such a perspective genuinely illuminates social reality and those in which another conceptual scheme might be more appropriate. Not all mobs are by any means anomic. The Negro riot in the urban United States may be an undirected, normless expression of deeply-felt discontent, or it may, on the other hand, be a purposeful attempt to change the policies and attitudes of the white majority. The first would be an example of mass anomic behaviour, the second of a social conflict situation. In this case, at least, it is apparent that we can only decide which interpretation is correct by an empirical examination of the relevant circumstances.

The concept of anomie

The most famous use of the term 'anomie' occurs in Emile Durkheim's classic studies of *Suicide* and *The Division of Labour in Society*. In both he attempts to link together certain types of pathological social behaviour with the disintegration or non-appearance of a normative structure integrating social activity. In the first of these studies, Durkheim argues that there is a particular type of suicide, anomic suicide, which corresponds to periods of social upheaval. He proceeds from the initial empirical regularity that suicide rates increase in periods of economic depression, and suggests that the commonsense view that this is a consequence of the increase in poverty must be mistaken.[5] Such a theory must be erroneous because firstly it is not the case that the most poverty-stricken regions and countries are those with the highest suicide rates, and secondly even more surprisingly, it is found that suicide rates also increase markedly in periods of rapidly increasing prosperity. This latter indicates that the factor involved in the increased suicide rates is not the absolute level of wealth, but the occurrence of rapid changes in the level.

Durkheim's assumption is that which we have seen is typical of the co-operative or conservationist metatheory, that man's potentially unlimited desires are held in check by the imposition of normative regulations of social conduct. Crises, whether economic or of a political or military nature, have the effect of temporarily disrupting this normative structure with the consequence of a higher incidence of uninstitutionalized activities like suicide. To use Durkheim's own phraseology, society has a 'collective conscience' by which it exercises moral restraint on its members . . .

> But when society is disturbed by some painful crisis or by beneficent but abrupt transitions, it is momentarily incapable of exercising this influence . . .
> In the case of economic disasters, indeed, something like a declassification occurs which suddenly casts certain individuals into a lower state than their previous one. Then they must reduce their requirements, restrain their needs, learn greater self-control. All the advantages of social influence are lost so far as they are concerned; their moral education has to be recommenced. But society cannot adjust them instantaneously to this new life and teach them to practise the increased self-repression to which they are unaccustomed. So they are not adjusted to the condition forced on them, and its very prospect is intolerable; hence the suffering which detaches them from a reduced existence even before they have made trial of it.[6]

The occurrence of anomic suicide in periods of crisis is an instance of the specification of the metatheory of normlessness that we have already mentioned. Here we find a restriction to periods and situations of crisis, only where they occur can there be noted a disintegration of social forms and a disruption of the 'collective conscience'. Durkheim's theory of suicide also delineates sections of the population more subject to suicide than others. This differential incidence of 'suicidal currents' is not described as anomic, but rather as a consequence of the differential degree of egotism or individualism manifested by social groupings. Egotist suicide is not a consequence of rapid alterations of normative expectations, but stems from the weakness of the normative patterns which bind some groups to the community as a whole. It is such normative weaknesses which explain the higher suicide rates of Protestants than Catholics, of the unmarried than the married, and the divorced than those whose marriages were terminated by human mortality.[7] In each case the explanation lies in the differential social solidarity expressed in the contrasting relationships. Protestantism leaves a man alone with his

God, whereas Catholicism binds him to the intermediary human institution of the Church. The social institution of marriage is regulated by a complex of normative expectations, whereas the unmarried are set loose in a moral jungle. Although it might appear that the divorced and widowed were similarly subject to a traumatic alteration in their life pattern, this is not entirely accurate. The death of a marriage partner does not involve the dissolution of the normative pattern involved in marriage, but rather is an expectation that is attached to the very enactment of the marriage contract. Divorce, however, involves the formal judicial dissolution of the normative pattern leaving both partners less socially integrated than previously.

The concept of normlessness would appear to be an illuminating one in both of these contexts of a sudden crisis leading to normative disorientation and of the differential degree of social integration experienced by individuals within the confines of varying social categories. In both cases it is a concept used for comparative purposes: in the former, a comparison between the ordered and stable structure and a temporary breakdown of that structure, and, in the latter, between a relatively integrated section of the populace and a relatively unintegrated section. The word 'relative' is vital in this context, since Durkheim does not mean to imply any absolute condition of normlessness, but is only attempting to suggest that some sections are better integrated than others. Not all the unmarried commit suicide, and not all those who go through the marriage ceremony avoid that fate. From the point of view of political analysis, the suggestion that crises may have a disorienting effect seems to be highly relevant. It would appear to be an empirical regularity that defeat in war is at least as potent a source of political revolution as sustained class conflict, however much this latter is promoted by a band of politically conscious intellectuals. In the terms suggested by Durkheim this would appear explicable as an anomic breakdown of social integration in face of a crisis of overwhelming proportions. This, it could be suggested, is a more cogent insight into what occurred in Russia in 1917 than the alternative theory that the workers were convinced by the realities of a capitalist war that they were unmercifully exploited and had 'nothing to lose but their chains'. There is little evidence to suggest that the great majority of the Russian population became markedly more politically conscious in the first three years of the war, but much to suggest that they became weary and disillusioned. The ideas of the old society ceased to be enshrined in the hearts and minds of the population, simply because they seemed incapable of making sense of the new circumstances, and although most had no positive commitment to the new order offered by Bolshevism, neither had they any interest in preserving Tsarism.

Durkheim's analysis of anomie arising from crisis situations seems to have a *prima facie* utility in political studies, but this is more dubious in respect of other points he makes about the concept. These points relate to the supposedly endemic character of anomic behaviour in the economic structure of modern industrial society. He argues:

> If anomie never appeared except, as in the above instances, in intermittent spurts and acute crisis, it might cause the social suicide rate to vary from time to time, but it would not be a regular, constant factor. In one sphere of social life, however— the sphere of industry and trade—it is actually in a chronic state.[8]

Durkheim's basic point is that 'economic progress has mainly consisted in freeing industrial relations from all regulation'.[9] Writing in the nineteenth century, he argued that religious constraints no longer applied to business activity, that the government had abdicated its responsibilities in this sphere, and that business itself no longer felt the need for self-restraint in terms of setting minimum standards and incomes. In theoretical terms, at least, commerce had been converted into a sphere in which anomie was the normal state of all interaction. As we might expect after this analysis Durkheim finds that the suicide rate is highest among those who exercise industrial and commercial functions. While not necessarily disputing either Durkheim's argument or conclusions, it is as well to be aware that they are in a sense pre-determined by his analytical perspective. Virtually every sociologist of the nineteenth century pointed to the disruptive social effects of unalloyed individualism and competition encapsulated in the dominance of economic market relationships. As Bramson notes, sociology inevitably focuses upon the importance of groups and group life.[10] Since the ideal of *laissez-faire* individualism was to make the individual autonomous of society, sociologists could not fail to deplore developments which seemed to realize this situation. In consequence, they frequently ignored the positive contributions made by the rise of modern industrialism. In sorrow for the presumed loss of the immediacy of social interaction in the context of the small community, they ignored the enormous gains in terms of the material standard of life that a market economy brought in its train.

Durkheim himself was not wholly pessimistic about the industrial progress brought about by the economic division of labour. In fact, he argued, it presupposed a new type and level of normative integration in society, which he called 'organic solidarity'.[11] The conditions of man's life in modern society are not merely regulated by the supply and demand of the market, but by normative regulations which enshrine the circumstances under which individuals are willing to co-operate in such a society. Such normative regulations are, for instance, provided in the institution of contract which sets out the conditions of sale and employment. Integration of this kind was by no means highly developed in Durkheim's day, and he sees disputes between labour and capital as an instance of a malfunctioning normative structure. To him such disputes were anomic, since they appeared to stem merely from a lack of regulation or normative patterning of the relationships between the two sides. There can be no doubt that to some extent this was true. It has already been mentioned that this century has seen a diminution of violent conflict between labour and capital through an institutionalization of the relationships between them. However, it would be completely inaccurate to see industrial disputes as being only a result of anomie. The institution-alization of procedures for the resolution of conflict does not mean that conflict between labour and capital has ceased, only that both sides have to a large extent abjured the most violent weapons of conflict. Durkheim is in error in attributing industrial conflict to anomie alone, since the demands of the two sides are related to their pursuit of disparate ends. Such a situation is not attributable to norm-lessness, but to an opposition of mutually incompatible goals. Perhaps a rough indicator of whether a model emphasizing anomie or con-flict is the most appropriate for the analysis of a given situation would be the persistence of the phenomena in question. A situation of normlessness is of necessity relatively short-lived. As a sociologist one must presume that individuals cannot live for long in a situation in which social ties are completely absent. On the other hand, and as Durkheim admits, the dispute between labour and capital is continu-ous and ubiquitous. To describe totally anomic behaviour as consti-tuting a relationship is logically contradictory, but it does not stretch the meaning of words to describe the dispute between labour and capital as a conflict relationship. In other words, where it seems appropriate to describe a social situation in terms of an enduring relationship, whether of co-operation or conflict, then an analysis using the concept of anomie would appear to be out of place.

A more recent use of the concept of anomie is contained in Merton's essay, 'Social Structure and Anomie', in which he argues that certain types of social structure may 'exert a definite pressure upon certain persons in a society to engage in non-conforming rather than conforming conduct'.[12] The basic argument is that there may be an incongruence between a society's culturally defined goals and the normatively patterned modes of achieving them, and that where such a situation exists, the individual must make the choice whether to pursue the ends or the means that are culturally prescribed.

This leads to a range of possible behaviour patterns described by the following table:

A Typology of modes of individual adaptation[13]

Modes of adaptation	Culture goals	Institutionalized means
1 Conformity	+	+
2 Innovation	+	−
3 Ritualism	−	+
4 Retreatism	−	−
5 Rebellion	±	±

We will briefly discuss the relevance to political studies of each of these modes of adaptation to normatively prescribed goals and means.

1 Conformity   This situation in which the individual conforms to social expectations in respect of both goals and means is obviously that emphasized by the functionalist metatheory. As Merton argues, such a situation is dependent for its maintenance on whether it provides satisfactions for individuals who adhere to both modes of normative patterning.

2 Innovation   In modern American society Merton suggests, there is an incongruity of goals and means which make these satisfactions very difficult to achieve. The American ethos offers a much higher stress on the goal of monetary success than on the appropriate institutionalized means of attaining this goal. There is, in other words, a greater emphasis on winning the game than on winning the game according to the rules. The innovator is the person who, because he is motivated by the prevailing cultural goal, but is unable in virtue of his social circumstances to achieve it by the prescribed means, resorts to less orthodox methods, such as criminal activity. As Merton notes, despite the success ethos, the American social structure largely prevents the poverty-stricken from rising in their station in life.

> Within this context, Al Capone represents the triumph of amoral intelligence over morally prescribed 'failure', when channels of vertical mobility are closed or narrowed in a society which places a high premium on economic affluence and social ascent for all its members.[14]

The relevance of this type of analysis to political studies may be illustrated by looking at a further disparity of cultural values and institutionalized means in American society. Almond and Verba point to the aspirational nature of the American political culture.

They argue that the typical American is more oriented to participant values (playing a part in decision-making) than he is to subject values (obeying governmental rulings).[15] These two sets of values may be visualized in terms of a goal and a means to attain it. Participation is a goal in the sense that it encapsulates the ideal of popular decision-making, and obedience to governmental rulings is the means through which such decisions are translated into effective policy. The emphasis on participant values may, however, cause frustration in those areas in which the political structure does not permit the realization of those values. Such frustration may lead to the innovator's appearing to achieve the decision-making without obeying the rules of the game. An analysis of this kind might be relevant to the manner in which individuals in the Southern States take it upon themselves to enforce the segregation of schools and other public places, and might be similarly applicable to the institution of lynch-law. In both cases what is happening is that individuals are literally taking the law into their own hands and ignoring the customary legislative and judicial means of achieving their ends.

3 Ritualism   This mode of adaptation occurs when the individual faced with the difficulties of achieving the culturally prescribed goals gives up the effort and merely goes through the motions of trying to be a success. Under these circumstances the means to the end becomes the end in itself, a ritual which must be performed to preserve the individual's self-respect. This form of adaptation is perhaps most common among the lower-middle class whose parents have typically exercised considerable pressures on their children 'to abide by the moral mandates of society'. The importance of this type of activity to political analysis is considerable. Modern industrial society is administered largely by monolithic bureaucratic organizations in which means for achieving goals are meticulously prescribed. When this emphasis on institutional means is associated with individuals who are prone to take such means as an end in themselves what is produced is the 'red tape syndrome'. Members of the public who are brought into contact with bureaucratic organizations often feel that the officials with whom they correspond are more concerned to obey the rules of their organization than to achieve the objects for which the organization was set up.[16]

4 Retreatism   This is less a mode of adaptation than a description of those who spurn the normal modes of social living. It includes tramps, psychotics, alcoholics, drug addicts and all those who inhabit the twilight zone on the social periphery, those who have passed beyond marginality to become outcasts. This mode of reaction to the culturally prescribed goals and means involves a genuine state of normlessness. The type of individual described may be said to constitute a categoric grouping, but one which because it has no basis whatsoever for meaningful and coherent interaction is never able to achieve a social actuality. This point is cogently made by Dahrendorf:

> Empirically, the formation of organized interest groups is possible only if recruitment to quasi-groups follows a structural pattern rather than chance. By this condition, the group described by Marx as the Lumpen-proletariat is excluded from conflict group formation. Persons who attain positions relevant for conflict analysis not by the normal process of allocation of social positions in a social structure, but by peculiar, structurally random personal circumstances, appear generally unsuited for the organization of conflict groups. Thus the lowest stratum of industrial societies is frequently recruited in manifold but structurally irrelevant ways: by delinquency, extreme lack of talent, personal mishaps physical or psychological instability, etc.[17]

From a political point of view those who retreat have little significance except as a symptom of the degree of anomie present in society and as a tool for any political group that can mobilize them.

5 Rebellion This situation occurs when individuals not merely withdraw their allegiance from culturally prescribed goals and institutionalized means, but counterpose to them an ideology which depicts the ideal of a new society that meets individuals' desires more fully. The Communist in western nations rejects the existing structure which does not accord the working class a reward commensurate with its labour and offers the image of a classless society in which such problems have been overcome. In contrast to retreatism, there seems no reason whatsoever for regarding this as an instance of anomic behaviour. Rather than finding a partial or complete lack of normative patterning, what is manifested is an opposition of goals, or, in other words, a conflict situation.

Situations of innovation and ritualism are less clear-cut than the complete normlessness of retreatism or the total opposition of norms presupposed by rebellion. It rather depends on one's interpretation of motives, whether one regards lynch-law in the Southern States as being an example of anomie or conflict. If the motivation is an over-emphasis on, and a misunderstanding of, the limits of citizen participation in the decision-making process, then anomie would appear to be the appropriate tool for analysis. However, if the motivation is basically an opposition to the normative pattern regulating the conduct of the Negro population, then it must be seen as an instance of social conflict. It would seem highly probable that in any real instance of such activity there is a mixture of these two motivations, and that consequently an analysis in terms of both conflict and anomie would be useful.

The politics of normlessness

As Bramson has noted, the European theory of mass society has its roots in the sociological analysis of social disintegration of which Durkheim's theory of anomie is but one strand. There are indeed very few works which make explicit the connection between the concept of anomie and the theory of mass society, which is perhaps an indication of how wide the gap is between those who study social processes and those who study politics.[18] Nonetheless, virtually every theory which discusses the phenomenon of mass society emphasizes, either explicitly or implicitly, its normlessness and lack of structuring. Daniel Bell in his critique of the idea of 'America as a Mass Society' summarizes the elements implicit in the mass concept, and in doing so makes this perfectly clear. Among these elements is a strong emphasis on the manner in which the enormous developments in modern transport and communications techniques, and the vast expansion of the economic division of labour, have brought men into a closer interdependence in which the implications of a single action may affect the entire community. At the same time, however, individuals have been sundered from their traditional social context.

The old primary ties of family and local community have been shattered; ancient parochial faiths are questioned; few unifying standards take their place. More important, the critical standards of the educated elite no longer shape opinion or taste. As a result, mores and morals are in constant flux, relations between individuals are tangential or compartmentalized rather than organic. At the same time greater mobility, spatial and social, intensifies concern over status. Instead of a fixed or known status symbolized by dress or title, each person assumes a multiplicity of roles and constantly has to prove himself in a succession of new situations. Because of all this, the individual loses a coherent sense of self. His anxieties increase. There ensues a search for new faiths. The stage is thus set for the charismatic leader, the secular messiah, who, by bestowing upon each person the semblance of necessary grace, and of fullness of personality, supplies a substitute for the older unifying belief that the mass society has destroyed.[19]

This summary has a triple emphasis: the destruction of old values, the conditions under which this occurs, and the vulnerability to totalitarian or authoritarian leadership such a situation implies.

The destruction of old values and the consequent normlessness is of course the feature of the mass society doctrine that links it with the concept of anomie. A number of writers in the conservative tradition have argued that the sheer growth of population in the nineteenth and twentieth centuries, the growth of the mass in a strictly numerical sense, is conducive to a weakening of values. Gustave Le Bon in his study of *The Crowd* suggests that the coming age will, as a result of population growth, improvements in communication and the extension of the suffrage, be one of the dominance of the crowd; 'the divine right of the masses is about to replace the divine right of kings'.[20] This is a highly pessimistic view, since Le Bon feels the crowd to be prone to violence and incapable of concerted thought. In the crowd individuals lose the normative constraints imposed by normal social life, and in their place subjective instincts come to the fore. Within the crowd the individual feels himself possessed of invincible power and his susceptibility to suggestion is increased.

> We see, then, that the disappearance of the conscious personality, the predominance of unconscious personality, the turning, by means of suggestion and contagion, of feelings and ideas in an identical direction, the tendency to immediately transform the suggested ideas into acts; these we see, are the principal characteristics of the individual forming part of the crowd. He is no longer himself but has become an automaton who has ceased to be guided by his will.[21]

Ortega y Gasset similarly argues that the mass has no values of its own. To him this is not a new phenomenon. The masses have always been with us, but two things distinguish the new situation, the growth in number of this section of the populace, and their increasing unwillingness to accept the values of the elite. In the past the mass-man was forced to accept an authority external to him in order to survive in a community in which the exigencies of nature still pressed heavily on man's shoulders. Today the advances of industry and science have removed this burden with the consequence that the 'mediocre' multitude wrongly feels itself capable of making social and political decisions.[22] A more modern theorist of mass society, Hannah Arendt, suggests a definition of the phenomenon which stresses its formlessness and the incapacity for groups to express their own interests. Masses are to be distinguished from classes by their lack of articulate goals; they are constituted of individuals who in virtue of sheer number or indifference cannot be inducted into the normal process of group life.[23]

What all these theorists have in common is a definition of the masses whose primary feature is their high degree of normlessness. To Arendt they are the Lumpenproletariat writ large, to Ortega y Gasset they are those unable to generate normative patterns for themselves, and to Le Bon they are those reduced from civilized codes of conduct to mere animal instinct. A mass society is one in which a large sector of the population behaves in a manner unconstrained by social patterns of expectation. It is necessary at this point to clear up a semantic difficulty presented by the conceptualization of a mass society. Insofar as the mass is distinguished by its normlessness, it is contradictory to speak of a mass society, since no society can exist where there is a total absence of normative patterning. The creation of a neologism to denote what is usually meant by 'mass society' seems unnecessary, but it should always be remembered that it involves a metatheoretical over-emphasis. The status of the concept is, as is invariably the case in denoting anomic states, a comparative one; it describes either an absence of normative constraints in a given part of the population or a temporary phenomenon of social disintegration. Kornhauser, in his book, *The Politics of Mass Society*, makes this error of arguing that a normless mass may be the basis for a form of social organization. He attempts to distinguish between *mass movements* and *totalitarian movements*, but in the nature of things is unable to offer any differentiating characteristics. Throughout much of his study the Communist party is referred to as, or implied to be, a mass movement, but elsewhere it is suggested that it is a totalitarian movement, since it has a coherently defined cadre structure, which may itself be defined for the infiltration of mass movements. It is by no means inappropriate to describe the Communist Party as an organization designed to induct the mass-man, but that Party's high degree of normative structuring makes it most inappropriate to call it a mass movement in any other sense. If any movement which attempts to induct the masses is called a 'mass movement', the distinction between that type of movement and the so-called 'totalitarian movement' becomes quite meaningless, since in this sense all totalitarian movements are also mass movements.

Despite the agreement of theorists of the mass society on the defining normlessness of the phenomenon, they proffer, as Kornhauser illuminatingly suggests, quite different explanations of the cause of this normlessness. On the one side, there are those aristocratic critics of mass society, like Ortega y Gasset and Le Bon, who stress that the danger stems from the loss of insulation of social and political elites. The crowd and the mass of the mediocre have entered the field of decision-making, and the elite has become accessible to the pressure of their demands, and is no longer able, in the manner advocated by Edmund Burke, to deliberate on issues and assess their merits in terms of the community interest. On the other side, there are those democratic critics, like Arendt, who suggest that the normlessness of the mass stems from the loss of insulation of the non-elite. They argue that modern developments, like the increased division of labour, the break-up of traditional community ties and the mass media, have led to the isolation of the individual. Instead of being organized into cohesive groups modern society is atomized and dissociated, and the individual is confronted by the naked power of authority. In these circumstances the non-elite is available for manipulation by elite leadership groups. Whereas the aristocratic view stresses the brutishness of the mass (Le Bon felt the crowd to be impulsive, irritable, suggestible, credulous, prone to exaggeration, intolerant, dictatorial, superficial and characterized by inferior reasoning power), the democratic view characterizes the mass by its anonymity, isolation and craving for leadership. Kornhauser combines these two perspectives to form his own definition of mass society: 'Mass society is a social system in which elites are readily accessible to influence by non-elites, and non-elites are readily available for mobilization by elites.'[24] On the basis of this characterization, he is able to set out the following typology of societal forms:

		Availability of non-elites[25]	
		Low:	High:
Accessibility	Low:	Communal society	Totalitarian society
of elites	High:	Pluralist society	Mass society

Kornhauser points out that their stress on the availability of non-elites makes the democratic critic confuse totalitarian and mass societies, whereas the emphasis of the conservative critic on the accessibility of the elite makes for a similar confusion between pluralist and mass societies. It would, for instance, be this latter type of confusion which makes Ortega y Gasset equate developments in the United States in the inter-war period with the processes which in Europe in the same period were making for fascism. Although both America and Europe at this time were similarly experiencing an increase in the ability of the common man to influence the decision-making process, there was nonetheless a significant difference between them. As Bell notes, the Americans are 'a nation of join-ers'.[26] They belong to a plethora of groups and organizations, whether they be trade unions, business groups, veterans organizations or whatever. In virtue of these plural interests and the implied adherence to group norms, they are at least to some extent insulated from elite manipulation.[27] At every point, elite demands are judged by the criterion of whether they foster or hinder the goals each group pursues. Such judgments may lead to co-operative or conflict rela-tionships with the elite, but there is no absence of criteria by which ends of action can be formulated; there is no anomie. As the authors of a study on the Co-operative movement have argued, the existence of democratic organizations of the kind listed above provide the hall-mark of the society which has not succumbed to mass influence. Participation in such associations

> provides training in democratic action and access to a forum
> of oppositional ideas, the toleration and dissemination of
> which are essential to democratic government. It offers a
> varied set of opportunities for the nurture and expression of
> politically and publicly directed energy. Democratic
> associations constitute the great intermediary foci of loyalties
> which distinguish the civil from the mass society in which
> nothing stands between the attachment of a man to his
> family and the nation state.[28]

It is precisely this lack of intermediaries between family and state which characterizes the politics of many of the European nations in the inter-war period. Those groups which existed were subordinated to the purposes of elite leaders who wanted to change society. To be a trade union member in Weimar Germany meant to support either the Social-Democratic, Catholic or Communist ideology, it did not mean supporting a body of normative regulations as to the conduct of industrial disputes. Indeed, industrial disputes were used as mere tools by both Nazis and Communists to achieve their own political ends. This was so, for instance, in the case of the Berlin tram-strike which was used by both parties to help unseat the SPD government in Prussia. Under these circumstances to be inducted into a group means not insulation from the elite, but subordination to its purposes. Whether the political situation existing in Weimar Germany is to be described as anomic or as a manifestation of social conflict depends rather on where one cuts in on the phenomenon. It is certainly the case that the leaders of the various ideological groupings concerned were aware of the situation as one of conflict, and it might be argued that insofar as their divergent ideologies expressed opposed interests of differing sectors of the populace this was an accurate appraisal.

If, on the other hand, one focuses on the individual with no firm group ties, and few criteria by which to judge the ideological views competing for his allegiance, then perhaps normlessness and mass society do seem to offer an appropriate perspective. Insofar as literature can be said to aid political understanding, it lends some weight to this latter view. 'I am a camera', says Christopher Isherwood in *Mr. Norris Changes Trains*, and the picture he takes of Germany in 1932–3 was amorphous and unstructured in the extreme. No one could be certain whether the Nazis or communists would gain the upper hand, and no one could identify what finally tilted the scales in one direction. A situation of this kind is quite atypical of social conflict, where one can analyse the strengths and weaknesses of the contending forces in terms of their objective interests. Individuals did not feel that they could control the course of events, and often they were not entirely certain what the events were. If from the point of view of the objective results of the situation in Germany in 1932–3 a conflict theory might appear the most insightful, then in terms of the internal dynamic of the situation, the way in which individuals experienced and reacted to their situation, the concept of mass society may also have something to offer. Once again, it may be argued, that an exclusive attachment to a single metatheoretical perspective obscures rather than clarifies our understanding of social and political reality.

The fact that, as we have seen, modern industrial progress does not *per se* cause mass behaviour, but may, as Bell notes, promote a pluralist group universe, constitutes a refutation to all those theories which attribute mass activity to such general processes as the division of labour, the group of bureaucratic organizations, urbanization, etc. Rather, as Kornhauser argues, and in so doing re-emphasizes the point Durkheim makes about anomic behaviour, the mass phenomenon stems from crisis situations. Such crises may arise from either discontinuities in authority or discontinuities in community.[29] The former type of crisis stems from a rapid change in a society's authority structure. The gradual growth of democratic ideas and practices which has been a phenomenon of the Anglo-Saxon nations has not proceeded everywhere in the same uninterrupted and even fashion. Indeed, the gradual and piece-meal fashion in which the British aristocracy relinquished their power to the emergent middle class was relatively atypical. More common, at least in Europe, was the aristocratic defence of privilege using all the weapons of suppression in their arsenal as a means to this end. The result was democracy through revolution, and the rapid overturn of the existing authority structure. In a single stroke all traditions were abolished by decree, the old normative patterns were declared inappropriate, and in their place new legitimations of authority and of law were instituted. Taking the concept of the rule of law in its widest most literal sense, we may distinguish between the results of these disparate forms of the development of democratic norms. Where in the Anglo-Saxon countries this development was gradual, the emerging norms were hallowed by a traditional cloak of legitimacy, but where the development took the form of a political crisis, it frequently led to a diminution of the legitimacy of law itself. An analysis in terms of discontinuities of authority, and the consequent weakening of norms sanctifying the rule of law, would seem to have an immediate relevance to the situation of many of the developing countries in which nationalist movements are attempting to supersede traditional forms of authority by revolutionary means. The difficulties and precariousness of establishing new legitimations after such an event are exemplified by the experience of the early years of the American republic. As Lipset notes, the American achievement of an ordered legitimacy was by no means inherent in the situation faced by the United States in its early years, but was very dependent on a mixture of luck and enlightened leadership.[30]

By discontinuities in community, Kornhauser means uneven and traumatic experiences of social change. It is not factors like industrialism and urbanization as such which cause social isolation and atomization into a mass, but when these processes occur unduly rapidly or affect one sector of a society more than another. Kornhauser notes, for instance, that, in contradiction to the Marxist prediction, Communist support does not come from the most urbanized countries, but from those in which the process of urbanization has been least even.

> There is a negative relation between the extent to which
> societies are urbanized and the size of Communist support,
> even though Communist parties get their major support from
> large cities within each country.[31]

The more extreme crises are in industrial society the greater will be the chance that mass movements will occur. From the fact that there is a high association between the level of unemployment and the increase in the extremist electorate, Kornhauser concludes that the greater the degree of economic depression in industrial society the greater will be the degree of social atomization and consequently of mass behaviour. This conclusion that mass behaviour and political extremism may stem from economic depression is an analogue of Durkheim's conclusion in respect of anomic suicide. Kornhauser does not, however, consider the possible political repercussions of a rapid increase in economic prosperity. As Durkheim noted, this is just as much a cause of a disorientation of normative expectations as depression. It might be suggested that some of the increased conflict manifested in the United States, and other highly affluent nations, in recent years might be attributable to this factor.

Just as the focus of attention of nineteenth century social theorists was directed to the phenomenon of conflict by the nature of their existential situation, so the perspective of the theorist of mass society is associated with one of the most significant political innovations of our time, the rise of totalitarianism. On this subject virtually all the critics of mass society are agreed. The unstructured mass and the normless individual, because of their lack of values are freely available for manipulation by the elite. Where social atomization does not exist naturally, Arendt argues, the proto-totalitarian leader creates it artificially by disbanding intermediary organizations and instituting a reign of terror which prevents the reassertion of any significant degree of social solidarity. The following passage summarizes this process:

> Mass atomization in Soviet society was achieved by the skilful use of repeated purges which invariably precede actual group liquidation. In order to destroy all social and family ties, the purges are conducted in such a way as to threaten with the same fate the defendant and all his ordinary relations, from mere acquaintances to his closest friends and relatives. The consequence of this simple and ingenious device of 'guilt by association' is that as soon as a man is accused, his former friends are transformed immediately into his bitterest enemies: in order to save their own skins, they volunteer information and rush in with denunciations to corroborate the non-existent evidence against him . . .[32]

Although not allowing the population any access to elite decision-making, the totalitarian polity involves an attempt to turn them into a literal mass incapable of any spontaneous action. This lack of ability to resist the regime is a theme examined by the Russian novelist, Daniel, in his short satire, *This is Moscow Speaking*. His story is set in the Soviet Union of the early 1960s in which he sees signs of the re-emergence of 'the cult of personality', the major failing for which Stalin was denounced at the Twentieth Congress of the C.P.S.U. in 1956. Daniel depicts a situation in which the Presidium of the Supreme Soviet declares a Public Murder Day on which 'all citizens of the Soviet Union, who have reached the age of sixteen, are given the right to exterminate any other citizen'.[33] The point of the story is an examination of individuals' reactions to this restoration of the period of the great purges. The general conclusion is the passivity of the reaction, individuals do not protest, at best they get drunk. Perhaps the most interesting observation is that people simply did not communicate their fears about Public Murder Day. It was not until months afterwards that even a group of close friends could discuss the matter, and even then it was with considerable apprehension. The extent of normlessness and inability to form social relationships in which the most potent of individual fears could be expressed, depicted by Daniel, is probably the maximum degree of ubiquitous anomie that can be contained within the framework of an on-going society. It is not that individuals are unable to form relationships around family, work situation and the prevailing conception of political reality, but rather that certain matters that fall outside the bounds of culturally prescribed 'progressive thought' must never be allowed to intrude on these relationships. To Arendt such a situation is maintained by the mechanisms of coercion, but in the vision of reality described by Daniel individuals long inured to this type of life are simply no longer able 'to think about the unthinkable'.

If the prospect of an atomized society of this kind is frightening, the most pessimistic aspect of the political theory of mass society is its emphasis that the normless masses welcome the opportunity to abdicate their freedom in this manner. Every word that Le Bon applied to the crown seems applicable to those who attended the Nuremburg rallies in the 1930s. His suggestion that the credulous and impulsive crowd could easily be won over by the aspiring leader who 'vigorously affirms, without ever attempting to prove, that his opponent is a scoundrel, having been guilty of several crimes' is one which Hitler might easily have endorsed.[34] What the anomic individual lacks is a framework of meaning in terms of which to interpret his experience. Part of that meaning may be supplied by the 'big lie' which in one simplistic phrase attributes all past trouble to Semitic contamination of the German 'Volk' or the stab-in-the-back by the Social Democrats, Moreover, the complement to the 'big lie' is the 'big promise' which offers a meaningful life as part of that greater social solidarity offered by the restoration of the grandeur of the Thousand Year Reich. That a metatheoretical emphasis on the normlessness of modern man should lead to this conclusion of the vulnerability of mass society to totalitarian take-over is hardly surprising. Anomie is in many ways analogous to the physical science concept of a vacuum, and what nature abhors so too does society. As a social animal man necessarily finds extended periods of normlessness acutely disturbing and is likely to take the first opportunity offered to reattain a structured social existence.

A concluding word

This discussion of normlessness, whether in relation to the sociological concept of anomie or the political theory of mass society, has had the same dual stress that has been apparent throughout this book. The first aspect of this stress has been the repeated argument that, despite their sometimes contradictory emphasis and frequent untestability, the different metatheoretical models we have examined all have a genuine role in promoting our understanding of social and political reality. Indeed much of what is contradictory can be eliminated if we think of the different models as concentrating on different levels of human behaviour. At a societal level there is an almost inevitable emphasis on the normative patterning which provides coherence for the societal structure. Given an awareness of the manifold sources of disruption that could threaten social existence, there would seem to be a very real area of social and political interest in the mechanisms that maintain a relatively stable framework of social meaning. Where the concentration is on behaviour in groups there is a contrasting tendency to emphasize what gives the group its unique identity, i.e. the interests which set it apart from other groups. Such an emphasis on social differentiation naturally leads to an analysis of the very real issues raised by group members' attempts to realize their interests, and the conflict and change entailed by such attempts. At the level of the individual there is an emphasis on the variety of disparate and confusing communications of which he is the subject. Perfect social integration is never possible because the individual can never come to terms with all that is expected of him, but some social structures and situations are more confusing than others, and the theorist of mass society is making the hardly outrageous point that the rapid social change of the present epoch is particularly conducive to situations of this type.

The other aspect that has been stressed throughout is that no empirical instance of social or political activity constitutes a pure example of stability, conflict or anomie. This is in a sense to repeat what has already been said. Because virtually all social and political phenomena have societal, group and individual aspects, they exhibit a combination of stable, conflicting and anomic elements. Certainly, our previous discussion has provided us with many examples of such combinations of differing types of interaction in real political situations. Institutionalized conflict and competitive situations involve a very clear combination of common normative patterns at the societal level and a conflict of interests at the group level. On the other hand, what has been described as 'ritualism' seems to involve a combination of common normative patterning in some respects and normlessness in others. The ritualist holds firm to the normative pattern regulating the means by which goals are to be attained, while abandoning the goals themselves as being too difficult for his individual attainment. Finally, the situations which have been described under the rubric of 'mass society' involve a combination of conflicting group interests and a high degree of anomie. The opposing elites have very different pictures of the type of society they desire as a replacement to hitherto existing society, and there is no question that their conflict has a real meaning in terms of the interests that will be served when one side is victorious. On the other hand, the individuals who find themselves between the lines are bombarded by a plethora of contradictory communications and social disorientation is a natural result. The complementary nature of the insight provided by the different metatheoretical perspectives is matched by the complementary nature of the phenomena they purport to illuminate. To become a functionalist, conflict theorist or theorist of mass society in an exclusive sense means to abandon an insight into the full diversity of social and political life.

Notes and references

Chapter 1

1 Francis Bacon, *Novum Organum*, Book 1, 1878.

2 'What, then, is noble abstraction? It is taking first the essential elements of the thing to be represented, then the rest in order of importance (so that wherever we pause we shall always have obtained more than we leave behind) and using any expedient to impress what we want upon the mind without caring about the mere literal accuracy of such expedient.' John Ruskin, *The Stones of Venice*, Smith, Elder, London, 1851–3.

3 This dismissive attitude to philosophy's role in political explanation is typified by its description as a 'tool subject' of political science, in contradistinction to those fields, a knowledge of which 'is essential to the student of political science to enable him to master the subject'. See W. A. Robson, *The University Teaching of Social Science: Political Science*, U.N.E.S.C.O., Geneva, 1955, p. 59.

4 This argument is a logical extension of Popper's view that the only scientific test of an hypothesis is to attempt to falsify it. See Karl Popper, *The Poverty of Historicism*, Routledge & Kegan Paul, London, 1961, pp. 130ff.

5 Thus Morris explains the high intensity of human aggression, manifested in warfare, by the superimposition of large-scale national organization on the fixed, and biologically determined, disposition to live in small face-to-face communities. See Desmond Morris, *The Naked Ape*, Cape, London, 1967.

6 For a description of this classificatory method in sociology, see John Rex, *Key Problems In Sociological Theory*, Routledge & Kegan Paul, London, 1961, pp. 4ff.

7 There were, of course, exceptions. Most notably Robert Michels, *Political Parties* first published in German in 1911.

8 Heinz Eulau, *The Behaviourial Persuasion in Politics*, Random House, New York, 1963, p. 3.

9 See Martin T. Orne and F. J. Evans, 'Social Control in the Psychological Experiment', *Journal of Personality and Social Psychology*, Vol. 1, 1965.

10 Since, in totalitarian regimes, and recently seemingly in more democratic ones, personal exposure appears to offer not inconsiderable risks, there would seem to be a need for an explanation of some kind.

11 See G. A. Almond and J. S. Coleman (eds), *The Politics of the Developing Areas*, Princeton University Press, New Jersey, 1960, Introductory chapter.

12 On the role of generational change in shaping electoral choice see David Butler and Donald Stokes, *Political Change in Britain*, Macmillan, London, 1969, pp. 44–64.

13 Lipset and Bendix outline five major lines of inquiry in the field of political sociology. They are voting behaviour, the concentration of economic power and political decision-making, ideologies, the study of political parties, voluntary organizations, oligarchy and political attitudes, and, lastly, government and bureaucracy. See Reinhard Bendix and S. M. Lipset, 'Political Sociology', *Current Sociology*, Vol. VI, 2, 1957, pp. 79–98.

14 Lewis Coser (ed.), *Political Sociology*, Harper & Row, New York, 1967, p. 5.

15 C. Wright Mills, *The Sociological Imagination*, Oxford University Press, New York, 1959, pp. 50–75.

16 If Ambrose Bierce, the author of *The Devil's Dictionary*, were alive today, he might well define psephology as the art of predicting the imminent demise of politicians by reading the entrails of electronic computers.

17 *The Sociological Imagination*, p. 52.

18 The great paradox in the development of electoral studies from their early fact-gathering stage is that while psephology's ability to explain and predict the nature of long-term electoral trends has improved (see *Political Change in Britain*, Part 3), its capacity to afford politicians sensible advice on their political prospects has increased hardly one iota.

19 See Paul R. Wilson and J. S. Western, 'Participation in Politics: A Preliminary Analysis', *Australian and New Zealand Journal of Sociology*, October, 1968.

20 See S. M. Lipset, *Political Man*, Doubleday, Anchor, New York, 1963; and Raymond Aron, 'Social Structure and the Ruling Class', *British Journal of Sociology*, Vol. I, 1, (March 1950) and Vol. I, 2, (June 1950).

21 See Floyd Hunter, *Community Power Structure*, University of North Carolina Press, 1953.

22 On this point see R. K. Merton, *Social Theory and Social Structure*, Free Press, New York, 1963, p. 98.

23 Where the empirical test of who holds power lies in the detailed analysis of given decisions, an inappropriate initial choice of decisions may destroy its whole relevance. See Robert A. Dahl, *Who Governs?*, Yale University Press, New Haven, 1961.

24 T. S. Eliot, *Old Possum's Book of Practical Cats*.

Chapter 2

1 Talcott Parsons (ed.), *Max Weber: The Theory of Social and Economic Organization*, Free Press, Chicago, 1947, p. 113.
2 Kurt H. Wolff (ed.), *The Sociology of Georg Simmel*, Free Press, Chicago, 1950, p. 122.
3 *Key Problems In Sociological Theory*, pp. 50–5.
4 W. J. H. Sprott, *Science and Social Action*, C. A. Watts, London, 1954, p. 9.
5 Claude Lévi-Strauss, *Les Structures Élémentaires de Parenté*, Presses Universitaires de France, Paris, 1949, Chapter v.
6 It would be interesting to know what would have happened to the discipline of Political Economy, which uses *Robinson Crusoe* as its archetypal example of economic co-operation, if Man Friday had not been so co-operative.
7 Emile Durkheim, *Suicide: A Study in Sociology*, Routledge & Kegan Paul, London, 1952, pp. 241ff.
8 For an explanation of the importance of perception in determining attitudes to poverty, see W. G. Runciman, *Relative Deprivation and Social Justice*, Routledge & Kegan Paul, London, 1966.
9 See Fritz Redl, 'Group Emotion and Leadership', *Psychiatry*, Vol. V, No. 4, November 1942, pp. 575–85.
10 See, for instance, von Hayek, 'Scientism and the Study of Society', parts I and II, *Economica*, vols ix and x.
11 *The Sociology of Georg Simmel*, pp. 145–70.
12 Emile Durkheim, *The Rules of Sociological Method*, Free Press, New York, 1966, p. 10.
13 Harold Fallding, *The Sociological Task*, Prentice-Hall, N.J., 1968, p. 63.
14 While Durkheim described the former condition as anomie, he denoted that in which the normative ties of the individual were weakened as 'egotism'. Despite the difference in causes, the results are similar for the individual, insofar as he is deprived of any coherent normative patterning of his social existence.
15 Without such normative regulation this would prove impossible. 'For where interest is the only ruling force each individual finds himself in a state of war with every other since nothing comes to mollify the egos, and any truce in this eternal antagonism would not be of long duration.' Emile Durkheim, *The Division of Labour in Society*, Free Press, New York, 1964, pp. 203–4.
16 For this usage, see Harry M. Johnson, *Sociology: A Systematic Introduction*, Routledge & Kegan Paul, London, 1961, pp. 21ff.
17 Adam Smith, *The Wealth of Nations*, first published in 1776.
18 This, of course, is the basis for Marx's famous distinction between a class 'in itself' and a class 'for itself'. See Karl Marx, *The Eighteenth Brumaire*, International Publishers Edition, New York, 1935, p. 109.
19 The idea of a Red-Headed League appears in Sir Arthur Conan Doyle's Sherlock Holmes stories. As one might imagine, the great detective rapidly discerns that so unlikely a group is really a cover for criminal activities.

20 E. C. Hughes, 'Dilemmas and Contradictions of Status', *American Journal of Sociology*, Vol. L, July 1944–May 1945.

21 See Muzafer, Sherif, 'Group Influences upon the Formation of Norms and Attitudes', in Maccoby, Newcomb and Hartley (eds), *Readings in Social Psychology*, Methuen, London, 1961, pp. 219–32.

22 Butler and Stokes, *Political Change in Britain*, pp. 155–7, argue for the opposite temporal sequence with Labour affiliation being a major determinant of trade union membership. This does not vitiate an analysis in reference group terms, since it might then be suggested that many working-class but non-Labour voters adopt the pattern of organizational membership that they consider appropriate to middle-class *mores*.

23 For a discussion of the deferential nature of the British political culture, see Richard Rose, *Politics in England*, Faber & Faber, London, 1965, pp. 40ff.

24 *Social Theory and Social Structure*, pp. 262–71.

25 R. K. Merton and A. S. Kitt, 'Reference Groups' in R. K. Merton and P. F. Lazarsfeld (eds), *Continuities in Social Research, Studies in the Scope and Method of 'The American Soldier'*, Free Press, Chicago, 1950, pp. 86–95.

26 This attitude is sublimely expressed for the poor, rather than by the poor, in the hymn 'All Things Bright And Beautiful' by Mrs. Alexander

> The rich man in his castle,
> The poor man at his gate,
> God made them, high or lowly,
> And order'd their estate.

Whether there is any significance in the fact that this was written in the same year as the Communist Manifesto I leave to the historians.

27 P. E. Converse and Georges Dupeux, 'Politicization of The Electorate in France and The United States' in *Political Sociology*, Harper & Row, New York, 1967, pp. 216–46.

28 Voltaire, *Candide*, Penguin, Harmondsworth, 1947, p. 20.

29 Phillip E. Slater, 'Social Bases of Personality' in N. J. Smelser (ed.), *Sociology: An Introduction*, John Wiley, New York, 1967, pp. 595–9.

30 For a biographical account of such an experience, see Evgenia S. Ginzburg, *Into The Whirlwind*, Collins, London, 1967.

31 'The Family Background of Harold Wilson', a B.B.C. interview with Brian Blake in Richard Rose (ed.), *Studies in British Politics*, Macmillan London, 1965.

32 G. A. Almond and S. Verba, *The Civic Culture*, Little, Brown & Co., Boston, 1965, pp. 266ff.

33 See C. J. Friedrich and Z. K. Brzezinski, *Totalitarian Dictatorship and Autocracy*, Harvard University Press, 1956.

34 R. A. Bauer, *The New Man In Soviet Psychology*, Harvard University Press, 1952, pp. 182–3.

35 Ron Hall, 'The Family Background of Etonians' in *Studies in British Politics*, Macmillan, London, 1965, p. 53.

36 See Erving Goffman, *Asylums*, Doubleday, New York, 1961.

37 Sociology has sometimes gone too far in suggesting that man's actions are totally determined by the external constraining influence of socialized normative patterns. This has provoked a reaction within sociology itself, which has suggested that the socialization perspective should not be taken so far as to obscure the psychological impulses which do exist (see D. H. Wrong, 'The Oversocialized Conception of Man', *American Sociological Review*, 26 April 1961, pp. 185–93), and has further insisted that it always be remembered that 'society is a human product' (see P. L. Berger and Thomas Luckmann, *The Social Construction of Reality*, Allen Lane, The Penguin Press, London, 1967, pp. 78–9).

Chapter 3

1 D. H. Lawrence, *Kangaroo*, Penguin, Harmondsworth, 1950, p. 324.
2 Stanislav Andreski, *Elements of Comparative Sociology*, Weidenfeld & Nicolson, London, 1964, p. 15.
3 Talcott Parsons, *Essays in Sociological Theory, Pure and Applied*, Free Press, Chicago, 1949, p. 18.
4 *Elements of Comparative Sociology*, p. 16.
5 See *Key Problems in Sociological Theory*, p. 17.
6 The illogicality stems from the fallacy of affirming the consequent. In terms of formal logic such an argument may be given the following form:

> If X is true then Y is true,
> But Y is true,
> Therefore X is true.

7 *Essays in Sociological Theory, Pure and Applied*, p. 19.
8 *Social Theory and Social Structure*, p. 98.
9 For an account of economic exchange in the Trobriands, see B. Malinowski, *Argonauts of The Western Pacific*, Routledge, London, 1932.
10 *The Poverty of Historicism*, pp. 133–4.
11 On this point, see Isidor Chein, 'Verity vs Truth in the Scientific Enterprise', invited address to the division of Philosophical Psychology at the Annual Convention of the American Psychological Association, 3 September 1967.
12 B. Berelson, *Content Analysis in Communications Research*, Free Press, Chicago, 1951.
13 For some of these criticisms, see Roger Brown, *Social Psychology*, Free Press, New York, 1965.
14 Alfred North Whitehead, *Science and The Modern World*, Macmillan, London, 1925, p. 107.
15 Karl Popper, *The Logic of Scientific Discovery*, Hutchinson, London, 1959, p. 38.
16 *Science and The Modern World*, pp. 60–1.
17 The process by which such models may be transformed into empirically-oriented propositions or hypotheses is discussed in Harold Fallding, *The Sociological Task*, op. cit.

18 Quoted by Arthur Koestler, *The Act of Creation*, Hutchinson, London, 1964, p. 242.

19 *The Division of Labour in Society*, p. 37.

20 Max Weber, *The Methodology of The Social Sciences*, Free Press, Chicago, 1949, p. 104.

21 That it frequently is what is maintained would appear to be the only explanation for some of the trivialities cited in Chapter 1.

22 *Social Theory and Social Structure*, pp. 103ff.

23 Percy Cohen, *Modern Social Theory*, Heinemann, London, 1968, p. 10.

24 P. A. M. Dirac, in *Scientific American*, Vol. 208, No. 5, May 1963.

25 Lewis A. Coser (ed.), *Sociology Through Literature*, Prentice-Hall, New Jersey, 1963, p. 3. Coser's introduction to this collection of literary extracts makes many of the points noted in this section, although there is perhaps a greater tendency to concentrate on the literary artist's acute eye in describing reality, rather than his ability to draw attention to novel relationships between the differing aspects of that reality.

26 On the concept of the vulnerability of insight see Bernard Lonergan, *Insight: A Study of Human Understanding*, Longmans, London, 1958, pp. 279ff.

27 Robert Bierstedt, 'Sociology and General Education' in C. H. Page (ed.), *Sociology and Contemporary Education*, Random House, New York, 1963, pp. 44–5.

28 Martin Esslin in his introduction to Henrik Ibsen, *An Enemy of The People*, Heinemann, London, 1967, p. xi.

29 Henry Fielding, *Tom Jones*, New American Library, New York, 1963, p. 116.

Chapter 4

1 Alex Inkeles, *What is Sociology?*, Prentice-Hall, New Jersey, 1964, pp. 28–46.

2 See T. D. Weldon, *States and Morals*, John Murray, London, 1962, pp. 98ff.

3 See Karl W. Deutsch, *The Nerves of Government: Models of Political Communication and Control*, Free Press, New York, 1963.

4 *Social Theory and Social Structure*, pp. 70–9.

5 Ibid., p. 75.

6 Gabriel A. Almond, 'A Developmental Approach to Political Systems', *World Politics*, 1965, pp. 183–214.

7 Ibid.

8 For a suggested probabilistic model of the polity, see Gabriel A. Almond and J. S. Coleman (eds), *The Politics of The Developing Areas*, Princeton University Press, New Jersey, 1960, introductory chapter.

9 Joseph Berliner, *Factory and Manager in the U.S.S.R.*, Harvard University Press, 1957.

10 For a political instance of conjectural history, see Friedrich Engels,

The Origin of The Family, Private Property and The State, Charles H. Kerr, Chicago, 1902.

11 B. Malinowski, 'Anthropology', *Encyclopaedia Britannica*, 1936, and reprinted in L. A. Coser and Bernard Rosenberg (eds), *Sociological Theory*, Macmillan, New York, 1957, p. 524.

12 On the Hobbesian problem of order, see Talcott Parsons, *The Structure of Social Action*, Vol. I, Free Press, New York, 1968, p. 89ff.

13 See Marion J. Levy Jr, *The Structure of Society*, Princeton University Press, 1952.

14 *Social Theory and Social Structure*, pp. 25–37.

15 'Anthropology' (*Encyclopaedia Britannica*) p. 528.

16 *Social Theory and Social Structure*, p. 32.

17 Carl G. Hempel, 'The Logic of Functional Analysis', in L. Gross (ed), *Symposium on Sociological Theory*, Harper & Row, New York, 1959, pp. 283–4.

18 K. Davis, 'The myth of functional analysis as a special method in sociology and anthropology', *American Sociological Review*, Vol. 24, No. 6, 1959, pp. 757–72.

19 Ernest Nagel, *The Structure of Science: Problems in The Logic of Scientific Explanation*, Harcourt, Brace & World, New York, 1961, Chapter iv.

20 See Talcott Parsons and N. J. Smelser, *Economy and Society*, Free Press, Chicago, 1956.

21 Eugene J. Meehan, *Contemporary Political Thought*, Dorsey Press, Chicago, 1967, pp. 165–6.

22 Raymond Aron, *France: Steadfast and Changing*, Harvard University Press, 1960.

23 For an analysis of the different types of systems models currently used in political studies, see Peter Nettl, 'The Concept of System in Political Science', *Political Studies*, October 1966, pp. 305–38.

24 Bernard Brown, *New Directions in Comparative Politics*, Asia Publishing House, London, 1962, p. 2.

25 Roy E. Jones, *The Functional Analysis of Politics*, Routledge & Kegan Paul, London, 1967, p. 57.

26 For an application of the functionalist model to international politics see David Easton, *A Systems Analysis of Political Life*, John Wiley & Sons, New York, 1965. For a critique of this approach, see M. B. Nicholson and P. A. Reynolds, 'General Systems, The International System, and The Eastonian Analysis', *Political Studies*, February 1967, pp. 12–31.

27 See, for instance, Morton A. Kaplan, *System and Process in International Politics*, John Wiley & Sons, New York, 1957.

28 A. K. Cohen, *Delinquent Boys: The Culture of The Gang*, Free Press, Chicago, 1955.

29 Talcott Parsons and E. A. Shils (eds), *Toward A General Theory of Action*, Harvard University Press, 1951, p. 53.

30 N. J. Smelser, *The Theory of Collective Behaviour*, Routledge & Kegan Paul, London, 1962, pp. 79ff.

31 For a use of this model of social change in understanding nationalist

movements, see Francis G. Castles, *Pressure Groups and Political Culture*, Routledge & Kegan Paul, London, 1967, pp. 19–31.

32 *The Functional Analysis of Politics*, p. 16.

Chapter 5

1 Karl Marx and Frederick Engels, *Manifesto of The Communist Party* (first published in 1848) in *Karl Marx and Frederick Engels: Selected Works*, Vol. I, Lawrence & Wishart, London, 1962, p. 34.

2 Ralph Dahrendorf, *Class and Class Conflict in An Industrial Society*, Routledge & Kegan Paul, London, 1959, p. 161.

3 Ibid., p. 162.

4 See Chester I. Barnard, *The Functions of The Executive*, Harvard University Press, 1938, pp. 163–75.

5 Lewis Coser, *The Functions of Social Conflict*, Routledge & Kegan Paul, London, 1956.

6 *Class and Class Conflict in An Industrial Society*, p. 164.

7 *Key Problems in Sociological Theory*, pp. 110–12.

8 *The Eighteenth Brumaire*, loc. cit.

9 This phenomenon is sometimes suggested to be an additional variety of the evaluative contamination of evidence discussed in Chapter 3, but there seems to be no logical reason why the fortuitous factors determining any scientist's focus of attention should influence his objectivity.

10 Herbert Spencer, *A System of Synthetic Philosophy*, Appleton, London, 1862–96.

11 It has been suggested that this reaction supplied the fundamental impetus for the classical tradition in sociology. See Robert A. Nisbet, *The Sociological Tradition*, Heinemann, London, 1966, pp. 9–16.

12 R. W. Mack and R. C. Synder in 'Approaches to the Study of Social Conflict: A Colloquium' in *Journal of Conflict Resolution*, Vol. I, No. 2, June 1957, p. 217.

13 *Class and Class Conflict in An Industrial Society*, p. 38.

14 Karl Marx, *Capital*, Dent, London, 1930.

15 *Science and The Modern World*, p. 52ff.

16 See *The Poverty of Historicism*, p. 16.

17 *Class and Class Conflict in An Industrial Society*, p. 39.

18 On the question of the separation of ownership and control see A. A. Berle and G. C. Means, *The Modern Corporation and Private Property*, Macmillan, New York, 1933.

19 On the connection between bureaucracy and the modern industrial order, see Max Weber, *Economy and Society*, Vol. 3, Bedminster Press, New York, 1968, pp. 956–1003.

20. S. M. Lipset in *Political Man* suggests that of fifty European, English-speaking and Latin American nations twenty-four may be considered unstable (p. 49). This survey excludes the African and Asian continents in which instability and conflict are endemic.

21 Karl Marx and Frederick Engels, 'Circular Letter to Bebel and others' in *Karl Marx and Frederick Engels: Selected Works*, Vol II, p. 485.

22 *The Communist Manifesto*, p. 45.

23 Ibid., p. 36.

24 *Comparative Sociology*, p. 265.

25 V. I. Lenin, *What is to be Done?*, Martin Lawrence, London, n.d., pp. 32–3.

26 Georges Sorel, *Reflections on Violence*, Free Press, Chicago, 1950, p. 91.

27 The description of this conception of power as being 'zero-sum' in nature is found in Talcott Parsons, 'The Distribution of Power in American Society' in *World Politics*, Vol X, No. 1, October 1957.

28 *Class and Class Conflict in An Industrial Society*, p. 176.

29 Ibid., p. 170.

30 *Capital*, Vol. III.

31 O. Dahlke, 'Race and Minority Riots: A Study in The Typology of Violence' in *Social Forces*, 1952.

32 Jessie Bernard, 'Parties and Issues in Conflict' in *Journal of Conflict Resolution*, 1957, p. 118.

33 See Allen Kassof, 'The Administered Society: Totalitarianism Without Terror' in *World Politics*, Vol. 16, July 1964, pp. 558–75.

34 On the manner of interest articulation in totalitarian systems, see Francis G. Castles, 'Interest Articulation: A Totalitarian Paradox' in *Survey*, No. 73, Autumn 1969, pp. 116–32.

35 Karl Marx and Frederick Engels, *The German Ideology*, Lawrence & Wishart, London, 1970, p. 64.

36 *The Functions of Social Conflict*, p. 152.

37 See Michael Young, *The Rise of The Meritocracy*, Penguin, Harmondsworth, 1961.

38 R. Dubin, 'Industrial Conflict and Social Welfare' in *Journal of Conflict Resolution*, 1957.

39 Ibid., p. 189.

40 *Class and Class Conflict in An Industrial Society*, pp. 179–240.

Chapter 6

1 Georg Simmel, *Conflict and The Web of Group-Affiliations*, Free Press, Chicago, 1955, p. 25.

2 *Sociology: A Systematic Introduction*, p. 577.

3 Leon Bramson, *The Political Context of Sociology*, Princeton University Press, 1961, p. 26.

4 *Key Problems of Sociological Theory*, p. 177.

5 For a criticism of Durkheim's use of suicide rates as an indicator of social states, see J. D. Douglas, *The Social Meanings of Suicide*, Princeton University Press, 1967.

6 *Suicide*, p. 252.

7 Ibid., pp. 153ff.

8 Ibid., p. 254.

9 Ibid.

10 *The Political Context of Sociology*, p. 16.

11 *The Division of Labour in Society*, pp. 111ff.

12 *Social Theory and Social Structure*, p. 132.

13 Ibid., p. 140.

14 Ibid., p. 146.

15 *The Civic Culture*, pp. 178–80.

16 This distinction between utilizing rules as a standard of behaviour and the pursuit of the substantive purposes of the organization is to be found in *The Theory of Social and Economic Organization*, pp. 184–6.

17 *Class and Class Conflict in An Industrial Society*, pp. 187–8.

18 One exceptional study which does make this link is S. de Grazia, *The Political Community*, Chicago University Press, 1952.

19 Daniel Bell, *The End of Ideology*, Free Press, New York, 1962, pp. 21–2.

20 Gustave Le Bon, *The Crowd*, T. Fisher, Unwin, London, 1903.

21 Ibid.

22 José Ortega y Gasset, *The Revolt of the Masses*, W. W. Norton, New York, 1932, pp. 10ff.

23 Hannah Arendt, *The Origins of Totalitarianism*, George Allen & Unwin, London, 1951, p. 311.

24 William Kornhauser, *The Politics of Mass Society*, Routledge & Kegan Paul, London, 1960, p. 39.

25 Ibid., p. 40.

26 *The End of Ideology*, p. 32.

27 For a contrary view, see C. Wright Mills, *The Power Elite*, Oxford University Press, New York, 1956.

28 G. N. Ostergaard and A. H. Halsey, *Power in Co-operatives*, Blackwell, Oxford, 1965, p. 67.

29 *The Politics of Mass Society*, pp. 129–58.

30 S. M. Lipset, *The First New Nation*, Basic Books Inc., New York, 1963, pp. 22–3.

31 *The Politics of Mass Society*, pp. 143–4.

32 *The Origins of Totalitarianism*, p. 323.

33 Yuli Daniel, *This is Moscow Speaking*, Collins and Harvill Press, London, 1968, p. 23.

34 See H. E. Barnes (ed.), *An Introduction To The History of Sociology*, University of Chicago Press, 1948, p. 490.

Bibliography

Almond, G. A., 'A Developmental Approach to Political Systems', *World Politics*, 1965.

Almond, G. A. and **Coleman,** J. S., (eds), *The Politics of the Developing Areas*, Princeton University Press, New Jersey, 1960.

Almond, G. A. and **Verba,** S., *The Civic Culture*, Little, Brown & Company, Boston, 1965.

Andreski, Stanislav, *Elements of Comparative Sociology*, Weidenfeld & Nicolson, London, 1964.

Arendt, Hannah, *The Origins of Totalitarianism*, George Allen & Unwin, London, 1951.

Aron, Raymond, *France: Steadfast and Changing*, Harvard University Press, Cambridge, Mass., 1960.

Aron, Raymond, 'Social Structure and the Ruling Class', *British Journal of Sociology*, 1950.

Bacon, Francis, *Novum Organum*, Book 1, Clarendon Press, Oxford, 1878.

Barnard, Chester I., *The Functions of the Executive*, Harvard University Press, Cambridge, Mass., 1938.

Barnes, H. E., *An Introduction To The History of Sociology*, University of Chicago Press, 1948.

Bauer, R. A., *The New Man in Soviet Psychology*, Harvard University Press, Cambridge, Mass., 1952.

Bell, Daniel, *The End of Ideology*, The Free Press, New York, 1962.

Bendix, Reinhard and **Lipset,** S. M., 'Political Sociology', *Current Sociology*, 1957.

Berelson, B., *Content Analysis in Communications Research*, Free Press, Chicago, 1951.

Berger, P. L. and **Luckmann,** Thomas, *The Social Construction of Reality*, Allen Lane, The Penguin Press, London, 1967.

Berle, A. A. and **Means,** G. C., *The Modern Corporation and Private Property*, Macmillan, New York, 1933.

Berliner, Joseph, *Factory and Manager in the U.S.S.R.*, Harvard University Press, Cambridge, Mass., 1957.

Bernard, Jessie, 'Parties and Issues in Conflict', *Journal of Conflict Resolution*, 1957.

Bierstedt, Robert, 'Sociology and Contemporary Education', *Sociology and Contemporary Education*, Random House, New York, 1963.

Blake, Brian, in *Studies in British Politics*, Macmillan, London, 1965.

Bramson, Leon, *The Political Context of Sociology*, Princeton University Press, New Jersey, 1961.

Brown, Bernard, *New Directions in Comparative Politics*, Asia Publishing House, London, 1962.

Brown, Roger, *Social Psychology*, Free Press, New York, 1965.

Butler, David, and Stokes, Donald, *Political Change in Britain*, Macmillan, London, 1969.

Castles, Francis G., *Pressure Groups and Political Culture*, Routledge & Kegan Paul, London, 1967.

Castles, Francis G., 'Interest Articulation: A Totalitarian Paradox', *Survey*, Autumn 1969.

Chein, Isidor, 'Verity vs Truth in the Scientific Enterprise', *American Psychological Association*, 3 Sept. 1967.

Cohen, A. K., *Delinquent Boys: The Culture of The Gang*, Free Press, Chicago, 1955.

Cohen, Percy, *Modern Social Theory*, Heinemann, London, 1968.

Converse, P. E. and Dupeux, Georges, 'Politicization of The Electorate in France and the United States', *Political Sociology*, Harper & Row, New York, 1967.

Coser, Lewis, *The Functions of Social Conflict*, Routledge & Kegan Paul, London, 1956.

Coser, Lewis A. (ed.), *Sociology Through Literature*, Prentice-Hall, New Jersey, 1963.

Coser, Lewis, (ed.), *Political Sociology*, Harper & Row, New York, 1967.

Dahl, Robert A., *Who Governs?*, Yale University Press, New Haven, 1961.

Dahlke, O., 'Race and Minority Riots: A Study in the Typology of Violence', *Social Forces*, 1952.

Dahrendorf, Ralph, *Class and Class Conflict in An Industrial Society*, Routledge & Kegan Paul, London, 1959.

Daniel, Yuli, *This is Moscow Speaking*, Collins and Harvill Press, London, 1968.

Davis, K. 'The Myth of Functional Analysis as a Special Method in Sociology and Anthropology', *American Sociological Review*, Vol. 24, No. 6, 1959.

De Grazia, S., *The Political Community*, Chicago University Press, 1952.

Deutsch, Karl, W., *The Nerves of Government: Models of Political Communication and Control*, Free Press, New York, 1963.

Douglas, J. D., *The Social Meanings of Suicide*, Princeton University Press, New Jersey, 1967.

Dubin, R., 'Industrial Conflict and Social Welfare', *Journal of Conflict Resolution*, 1957.

Durkheim, Emile, *Suicide: A Study in Sociology*, Routledge & Kegan Paul, London, 1952.

Durkheim, Emile, *The Division of Labour in Society*, Free Press, New York, 1964.
Durkheim, Emile, *The Rules of Sociological Method*, Free Press, New York, 1966.
Easton, David, *A Systems Analysis of Political Life*, John Wiley & Sons, New York, 1965.
Engels, Friedrich, *The Origin of The Family, Private Property and the State*, Charles H. Kerr, Chicago, 1902.
Esslin, Martin, *An Enemy of the People*, Heinemann, London, 1967.
Eulau, Heinz, *The Behaviourial Persuasion in Politics*, Random House, New York, 1963.
Fallding, Harold, *The Sociological Task*, Prentice-Hall, New Jersey, 1968.
Fielding, Henry, *Tom Jones*, New American Library, New York, 1963.
Friedrich, C. J. and **Brzezinski,** Z. K., *Totalitarian Dictatorship and Autocracy*, Harvard University Press, Cambridge, Mass., 1956.
Ginzburg, Evgenia S., *Into the Whirlwind*, Collins, London, 1967.
Goffman, Erving, *Asylums*, Doubleday, New York, 1961.
Hall, Ron, 'The Family Background of Etonians' in *Studies in British Politics*, Macmillan, London, 1965.
Hempel, Carl G., *Symposium on Sociological Theory*, Harper & Row, New York, 1959.
Hughes, E. C., 'Dilemmas and Contradictions of Status', *American Journal of Sociology*, July 1944–May 1945.
Hunter, Floyd, *Community Power Structure*, University of North Carolina Press, 1953.
Inkeles, Alex, *What is Sociology?*, Prentice-Hall, New Jersey, 1964.
Johnson, Harry M., *Sociology: A Systematic Introduction*, Routledge & Kegan Paul, London, 1961.
Jones, Roy E., *The Functional Analysis of Politics*, Routledge & Kegan Paul, London, 1967.
Kaplan, Morton A., *System and Process in International Politics*, John Wiley & Sons, New York, 1957.
Kassof, Allen, 'The Administered Society: Totalitarianism Without Terror', *World Politics*, Vol. 16, July 1964.
Koestler, Arthur, *The Act of Creation*, Hutchinson, London, 1964.
Kornhauser, William, *The Politics of Mass Society*, Routledge & Kegan Paul, London, 1960.
Lawrence, D. H., *Kangaroo*, Penguin, Harmondsworth, 1950.
Le Bon, Gustave, *The Crowd*, T. Fisher, Unwin, London, 1903.
Lenin, V. I., *What is to be Done?* Martin Lawrence, London, n.d.
Lévi-Strauss, Claude, *Les Structures Élémentaires de Parenté*, Presses Universitaires de France, Paris, 1949.
Levy, Marion J., Jr., *The Structure of Society*, Princeton University Press, New Jersey, 1952.
Lipset, S. M., *Political Man*, Doubleday, Anchor, New York, 1963.
Lipset, S. M., *The First New Nation*, Basic Books Inc., New York, 1963.
Lonergan, Bernard, *Insight: A Study of Human Understanding*, Longmans, London, 1958.

Mack, R. W. and **Synder, R. C.**, 'Approaches to the Study of Social Conflict: A Colloquium', *Journal of Conflict Resolution*, Vol. 1, No. 2, June 1957.

Malinowski, B., *Argonauts of the Western Pacific*, Routledge, London, 1932.

Malinowski, B., 'Anthropology', *Encyclopaedia Britannica*, 1936.

Marx, Karl, *Capital*, Dent, London, 1930.

Marx, Karl, *The Eighteenth Brumaire*, International Publishers Edition, New York, 1935.

Marx, Karl and **Engels, Frederick**, *Circular Letter to Bebel and Others*, Lawrence & Wishart, London, 1962.

Marx, Karl and **Engels, Frederick**, *Manifesto of The Communist Party*, Lawrence & Wishart, London, 1962.

Marx, Karl and **Engels, Frederick**, *The German Ideology*, Lawrence & Wishart, London, 1970.

Meehan, Eugene J., *Contemporary Political Thought*, Dorsey Press, Chicago, 1967.

Merton, R. K., *Social Theory and Social Structure*, Free Press, New York, 1963.

Merton, R. K. and **Kitt, A. S.**, 'Reference Groups' in Merton, R. K., and Lazarsfeld, P. F., *Continuities in Social Research, Studies in the Scope and Method of 'The American Soldier'*, Free Press, Chicago, 1950.

Mills, C. Wright, *The Power Elite*, Oxford University Press, New York, 1956.

Mills, C. Wright, *The Sociological Imagination*, Oxford University Press, New York, 1959.

Morris, Desmond, *The Naked Ape*, Cape, London, 1967.

Nagel, Ernest, *The Structure of Science: Problems in The Logic of Scientific Explanation*, Harcourt, Brace & World, New York, 1961.

Nettl, Peter, 'The Concept of System in Political Science', *Political Studies*, Oct. 1966.

Nicholson, M. B. and **Reynolds, P. A.**, 'General Systems, The International System, and the Eastonian Analysis', *Political Studies*, 1967.

Nisbet, Robert A., *The Sociological Tradition*, Heinemann, London, 1966.

Orne, Martin T. and **Evans, F. J.** 'Social Control in the Psychological Experiment', *Journal of Personality and Social Psychology*. Vol. 1, 1965.

Ortega Y Gasset, José, *The Revolt of the Masses*, W. W. Norton, New York, 1932.

Ostergaard, G. N. and **Halsey, A. H.**, *Power in Co-operatives*, Blackwell, Oxford, 1965.

Parsons, Talcott, *Max Weber: The Theory of Social and Economic Organisation*, Free Press, Chicago, 1947.

Parsons, Talcott, *Essays in Sociological Theory, Pure and Applied*, Free Press, Chicago, 1949.

Parsons, Talcott, 'The Distribution of Power in American Society', *World Politics* Vol. X, No. 1, 1957.

Parsons, Talcott, *The Structure of Social Action*, Vol. 1, Free Press, New York, 1968.

Parsons, Talcott and **Shils,** E. A. (eds), *Toward a General Theory of Action,* Harvard University Press, Cambridge, Mass., 1951.

Parsons, Talcott, and **Smelser,** N. J., *Economy and Society,* Free Press, Chicago, 1956.

Popper, Karl, *The Logic of Scientific Discovery,* Hutchinson, London, 1959.

Popper, Karl, *The Poverty of Historicism,* Routledge & Kegan Paul, London, 1961.

Redl, Fritz, 'Group Emotion and Leadership', *Psychiatry,* Vol. V, No. 4, Nov. 1942.

Rex, John, *Key Problems in Sociological Theory,* Routledge & Kegan Paul, London, 1961.

Robson, W. A., *The University Teaching of Social Science: Political Science,* U.N.E.S.C.O., Geneva, 1955.

Rose, Richard, *Politics in England,* Faber & Faber, London, 1965.

Runciman, W. G., *Relative Deprivation and Social Justice,* Routledge & Kegan Paul, London, 1966.

Ruskin, John, *The Stones of Venice,* Smith, Elder, London, 1851–3.

Sherif, Muzafer, 'Group Influences upon the Formation of Norms and Attitudes' in Maccoby, Newcomb and Hartley (eds), *Readings in Social Psychology,* Methuen, London, 1961.

Simmel, Georg, *Conflict and The Web of Group-Affiliations,* Free Press, Chicago, 1955.

Slater, Phillip E., 'Social Bases of Personality' in Smelser, N. J., (ed.), *Sociology: An Introduction,* John Wiley, New York, 1967.

Smelser, N. J., *The Theory of Collective Behaviour,* Routledge & Kegan Paul, London, 1962.

Sorel, Georges, *Reflections on Violence,* Free Press, Chicago, 1950.

Spencer, Herbert, *A System of Synthetic Philosophy,* Appleton, London, 1896.

Sprott, W. J. H., *Science and Social Action,* C. A. Watts, London, 1954.

Voltaire, *Candide,* Penguin, Harmondsworth, 1947.

Von Hayek, 'Scientism and the Study of Society', Parts I and II, *Economica,* vols. ix and x

Weber, Max, *The Methodology of The Social Sciences,* Free Press, Chicago, 1949.

Weber, Max, *Economy and Society,* Vol. 3, Bedminster Press, New York, 1968.

Weldon, T. D., *States and Morals,* John Murray, London, 1962.

Whitehead, Alfred North, *Science and The Modern World,* Macmillan, London, 1925.

Wilson, Paul R. and **Western,** J. S., 'Participation in Politics: A Preliminary Analysis', *Australian and New Zealand Journal of Sociology,* Oct. 1968.

Wolff, Kurt H. (ed.), *The Sociology of Georg Simmel,* Free Press, Chicago, 1950.

Wrong, D. H., 'The Oversocialised Conception of Man', *American Sociological Review,* 26, April 1961.

Young, Michael, *The Rise of the Meritocracy,* Penguin, Harmondsworth, 1961.

Index